The African American Religious Experience

Lucent Library of Black History

Other titles in this series:

A Dream Defferred: The Jim Crow Era

The Fight Renewed: The Civil Rights Movement

The Harlem Renaissance

A Peculiar Institution: Slavery in the Plantation South

Ray Charles and the Birth of Soul

A History of Free Blacks in America

Marcus Garvey and the Back to Africa Movement

Harriet Tubman and the Underground Railroad

From Ragtime to Hip-Hop: A Century of Black American Music

Jackie Robinson and the Integration of Baseball

Lynching and Murder in the Deep South

Separate but Equal: The Desegregation of America's Schools

Slave Rebellions

The African American Religious Experience

Lucent Library of Black History

Stephen Currie

LUCENT BOOKS

A part of Gale, Cengage Learning

GALE
CENGAGE Learning

Detroit • New York • San Francisco • New Haven, Conn • Waterville, Maine • London

GALE
CENGAGE Learning

© 2008 Gale, a part of Cengage Learning

For more information, contact
Lucent Books
27500 Drake Rd.
Farmington Hills, MI 48331-3535
Or you can visit our Internet site at gale.cengage.com

LIBRARY OF CONGRESS CATALOGING-IN-PUBLICATION DATA

Currie, Stephen, 1960–
  The African American religious experience / by Stephen Currie.
    p. cm. — (Lucent library of Black history)
  Includes bibliographical references and index.
  ISBN 978-1-4205-0006-6 (hardcover)
  1. African Americans—Religion. I. Title.
  BR563.N4C87 2007
  200.89'96073—dc22

                                                                2007022998

ISBN-10: 1-4205-0006-6

Printed in the United States of America
2 3 4 5 6 7 12 11 10 09 08

Contents

Foreword   6

Introduction
Black History, Black Religion   8

Chapter One
Slave Religion   14

Chapter Two
The Rise of the Black Church   29

Chapter Three
Black Sacred Music   44

Chapter Four
African American Islam   57

Chapter Five
Religion and Civil Rights   72

Afterword
African American Religion Today   86

Notes   93
For More Information   97
Index   99
Picture Credits   103
About the Author   104

Foreword

It has been more than 500 years since Africans were first brought to the New World in shackles, and over 140 years since slavery was formally abolished in the United States. Over 50 years have passed since the fallacy of "separate but equal" was obliterated in the American courts, and some forty years since the watershed Civil Rights Act of 1965 guaranteed the rights and liberties of all Americans, especially those of color. Over time, these changes have become celebrated landmarks in American history. In the twenty-first century, African American men and women are politicians, judges, diplomats, professors, deans, doctors, artists, athletes, business owners, and home owners. For many, the scars of the past have melted away in the opportunities that have been found in contemporary society. Observers such as Peter N. Kirsanow, who sits on the U.S. Commission of Civil Rights, point to these accomplishments and conclude, "The growing black middle class may be viewed as proof that most of the civil rights battles have been won."

In spite of these legal victories, however, prejudice and inequality have persisted in American society. In 2003, African Americans comprised just 12 percent of the nation's population, yet accounted for 44 percent of its prison inmates and 24 percent of its poor. Racially motivated hate crimes continue to appear on the pages of major newspapers in many American cities. Furthermore, many African Americans still experience either overt or muted racism in their daily lives. A 1996 study undertaken by Professor Nancy Krieger of the Harvard School of Public Health, for example, found that 80 percent of the African American participants reported having experienced racial discrimination in one or more settings, including at work or school, applying for housing and medical care, from the police or in the courts, and on the street or in a public setting.

It is for these reasons that many believe the struggle for racial equality and justice is far from over. These episodes of discrimination threaten to shatter the illusion that America has completely overcome its racist past, causing many black Americans to become increasingly frustrated and confused. Scholar and writer Ellis Cose has described this splintered state in the following way: "I have done everything I was supposed to do. I have stayed out of trouble with the law, gone to the right schools, and worked myself nearly to death. What more do they want? Why in God's name won't they accept me as a full human being?" For Cose and others, the struggle for equality and justice has yet to be fully achieved.

In many subtle yet important ways the traumatic experiences of slavery and segregation continue to inform the way race is discussed and experienced in the twenty-first century. Indeed, it is possible that America will always grapple with the fallout from its distressing past. Ulric Haynes, dean of the Hofstra University School of Business has said, "Perhaps race will always matter, given the historical circumstances under which we came to this country." But studying this past and understanding how it contributes to present-day dialogues about race and history in America is a critical component of contemporary education. To this end, the Lucent Library of Black History offers a thorough look at the experiences that have shaped the black community and the American people as a whole. Annotated bibliographies provide readers with ideas for further research, while fully documented primary and secondary source quotations enhance the text. Each book in the series explores a different episode of black history; together they provide students with a wealth of information as well as launching points for further study and discussion.

Black History, Black Religion

The history of black people in America contains more than its share of tragedy. Indeed, African American history was born in violence. Whereas people from other nations made their own decisions to come to America, Africans were given no such choice. Instead, they were brought to North America as slaves. Some were captured on the African continent by white sea captains; others were taken prisoner by rival African groups and sold to European slave traders. Transported across the sea under horrible conditions, these new Americans were then sold to the highest bidder and forced to labor without pay.

The American system of slavery, by any standard, was brutal and unjust. Black slaves—and all American slaves were black—lived entirely at the whim of their masters. They could be sold to another owner whenever their masters chose, and their family members were not always sold along with them. Black slaves were routinely overworked and frequently beaten. Sometimes they were abused so badly that they died. Nonetheless, slaves had no rights that their white owners were required to respect. A slave was viewed, instead, rather like a horse or a plow—as an object, not as a human being.

Though slavery spread throughout the British North American colonies during the 1600s, it was neither widespread nor especially profitable in the North. Following the American Revolution and the establishment of the United States as an independent nation, most northern states abolished slavery altogether. But in the South the institution of slavery flourished. By 1860 the region was home to about 4 million enslaved men, women, and children. Though there were free blacks throughout the country as well, the slaves made up the great bulk of African Americans of the time.

An advertisement from 1780 announces an upcoming slave auction.

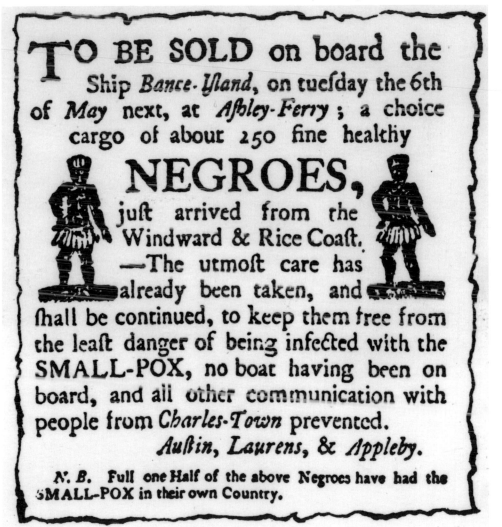

After Slavery and Beyond

In 1865, following the close of the Civil War, slavery did finally come to an end. Freedom, though, did not automatically elevate the status of African Americans. Poor and unskilled, the former slaves were looked down upon by most American whites. Laws restricted their movements and their ability to take part in government. Discriminated against in jobs, education, and housing, African Americans lagged behind their white counterparts in every measure of wealth and quality of life.

It took almost a century after the Civil War for this situation to begin to change. During the 1950s and 1960s thousands of African Americans banded together to demand their civil rights—the rights due to them as members of society. They worked for an end to segregation—the system of separating the races in schools and elsewhere—and they worked to gain and protect voting privileges for blacks. The civil rights movement brought political and social change to millions of American blacks, but it brought more, too. The success of the movement raised the spirits of African Americans across the country and helped them take pride in their heritage and their achievements.

Even the civil rights movement, however, could not erase all the problems faced by African Americans. Despite the gains of the civil rights era, blacks today struggle as a group in ways that Americans of most other races do not. African Americans are poorer than people of other races, for example, and they are more likely to leave high school before graduating. They are more likely to be imprisoned. And they are more likely to die violently. While new opportunities have helped many American blacks move into the middle class and beyond, many other African Americans have made little progress.

Yet, the harsh realities of African American history notwithstanding, most blacks have never given up hope for a brighter future. Many slaves spoke longingly of freedom; some ran away from their masters or even plotted revolt in order to get it. In the early twentieth century tens of thousands of poor black southern farmers moved north to find jobs, hoping to start over in a place where they felt racism would be less virulent. The civil rights activists of the 1950s and 1960s never lost sight of what a better, fairer world could look like. And today, too, many blacks continue to work tirelessly to create a society in which all African Americans can reach their full potential.

Religious Faith

The emphasis on hope among African Americans comes from many sources, but one of the most significant of these is religion. From the beginning of African American history, religious faith has played a vital role in African American life. It has been a comfort and an inspiration, a refuge and a source of strength. Religious faith

A hand-colored woodcut shows African Americans taking part in a prayer meeting.

has provided African Americans—from the earliest African slaves on the North American continent to black worshippers at megachurches today—with meaning and joy in a world that often seems to lack both. Over the years, black religious expression has offered a counterweight to racism, slavery, and modern urban blight.

African American religion has taken many different forms through history. For the most part, African Americans have been Protestant Christians. Traditionally, most of these Protestants have joined either the Methodist or Baptist denominations, though a growing number belong to Pentecostal churches. During the early years of slavery, however, African religions were common among North American slaves, and Christianity was virtually unknown. And Islam is growing steadily in its appeal to African Americans today.

Christianity, Islam, and traditional African faiths are all different in important and obvious ways. Still, different varieties of African American religious expression share certain characteristics. One is a concern for the entire black community. African Americans of faith have traditionally pooled their resources to provide for the neediest among them. The civil rights movement, which stemmed in large part from the convictions of religious African Americans, was at heart dedicated to the improvement of all blacks, religious or not. Christian congregations of various denominations have established literacy programs and fed the hungry. Islamic mosques have developed ministries to young black prisoners. Throughout black history, outreach has been a vital part of black religion.

Another characteristic common to black religious groups is the connection of faith to daily life. For most African Americans, now and in the past, worship is not confined to Sunday morning church services or Wednesday evening prayer meetings. Rather, blacks tend to view religious expression as an integral part of being human. Life, in this view, is a constant opportunity to offer praise and thanks to a higher power. Former slave Elizabeth Ross Hite complained about her master, who as she put it "jest wanted us to be Catholicses on Sunday. . . . [He] didn't want us shoutin' and moanin' all day long, but you gotta shout and moan if you wants to be saved."[1]

Perhaps most important of all, religion has consistently served to uplift the hearts and souls of American blacks. When the forces of the world have seemed to be arrayed against African Americans, faith in God has often reminded blacks that they, too, are loved—and as worthy as anyone else of entering heaven. As a slave preacher used to tell his congregations after his sermons were over, "Remember, you are not niggers! You are not slaves! You are children of God!"[2] Over the years, that message has resounded again and again for African Americans. More than any other, perhaps, it has been at the heart of what it means to be an African American of faith.

Chapter One

Slave Religion

The roots of African American religion lie in the earliest years of British settlement in the New World. The first Africans in Britain's North American colonies arrived in Jamestown, Virginia, in 1619. After that the number of blacks steadily increased. By 1650 thousands of people of African descent lived in the colonies. When the American Revolution broke out in 1775, hundreds of thousands more lived in the colonies, and at the start of the Civil War in 1861, African Americans numbered well over 4 million.

The vast majority of these early African Americans were slaves. Abused, mocked, and bound to their masters for life, they were the victims of one of the cruelest and most dehumanizing institutions in American history. Yet, all its wretchedness notwithstanding, the slave system also created the foundations of African American religious expression as it exists today.

The First Slaves

Africa was the home continent of the first colonial slaves. Most of these people originally came from a stretch of land in West

Africa that runs from present-day Senegal east and south along the coastline to Angola. A few early slaves were captured by white slave traders who roamed the countryside looking for human cargo. More, however, were obtained when Europeans purchased them from powerful local rulers. African peoples were often at war with one another, and prisoners taken during these conflicts were quite often sold to whites.

A few of these early slaves were transported from Africa directly to the British North American colonies. A large majority, however, were shipped first to the islands of Cuba and Hispaniola in the Caribbean, where slavery was already well established. There, they were put to work on sugar plantations. Later, slave

Captured Africans are marched toward slavery.

traders purchased some of these men, women, and children and transported them to Virginia, South Carolina, or Massachusetts to feed the growing North American appetite for slaves.

Whether they came directly from their homeland or made a stop in the Caribbean, however, the first North American slaves belonged to Africa and its culture. They were used to traditional African foods and clothing; they spoke African languages and were familiar with the landscapes and weather patterns of their home continent. The New World, in contrast, offered little that was familiar. Worse, most slaves brought to the British colonies were separated from friends and family along the way. As a result, the slaves perceived North America as strange, frightening, and lonely.

Nor could the slaves do much to make themselves feel at home in the New World. Few foods of their homelands were native to North America. Slaves typically had no opportunity to make their own clothing or houses, even if they could have used American materials to imitate African sewing methods and construction styles. It was not possible for slaves to reconstitute the clans and family groupings that formed the basis of traditional West African society. Even language could not persist for long. Since captives were drawn from all over western Africa, slaves often could not communicate with fellow workers in their native tongues.

African Religion

In the area of religion, however, the early slaves' connections with African culture did remain strong. The slaves brought the rituals, prayers, and gods of Africa with them to the New World. Religion offered them a connection to the past that little else could provide. At the same time, the slaves' faith could offer them hope even under the appalling circumstances of their capture and enslavement. Traditional African religion comforted the slaves on the long and dreadful journey across the Atlantic and gave them courage and strength as they began their new lives in America.

Though some West Africans of the 1600s were Muslims, most practiced one of a variety of traditional religions. These faiths differed from one another in several respects, but they also shared some important features. Most, for example, believed in a single supreme being. Among the Yoruba people of Nigeria, this role was filled by a deity known as Olorun—a name that translates lit-

Villagers gather to watch a dancer perform a West African religious ceremony.

erally to "owner of the sky." Other peoples used different names and probably pictured their supreme being differently. Still, the belief in a single creator god was common to traditional faiths of the region.

At the same time, West African religion accepted the existence of dozens of lesser spirits, each with certain responsibilities and characteristics. West Africans believed, moreover, that these spirits played important roles in people's lives. Neither distant nor removed from human experience, they were ever present in nature. Many of these spirits were understood to be the ancestors of believers. Members of traditional African religions frequently offered prayers to the spirits, hoping to influence them to act on their behalf.

Traditional African religion was marked by other ideas and rituals, too. "Spirits, though invisible," writes one historian, "took form in human mediums, as well as in masks [and] medicines . . . that gave people physical access to their spiritual power."[3] Religious leaders frequently went into trances as they channeled these spirits. Animal sacrifices were also common in traditional African faiths, and worship services often incorporated music, chanting, and drums.

Not all of these features made their way to the British colonies intact. Many groups of slaves, for example, found themselves without experienced religious leaders, forcing them to rely on a slave with an imperfect knowledge of the faith and its rituals. North American plants and animals were not the same as those

Slave Worship

◼

Religious expression among slaves depended in part on who organized and led the worship. Often, slaves went to services that were planned and run by white preachers. These preachers typically instructed blacks to follow the Ten Commandments, but spoke of little else. One former slave summed up the message of these sermons as follows: "Serve your masters. Don't steal your master's turkey. Don't steal your master's chickens. Don't steal your master's hogs. Don't steal your master's meat. Do whatsomever your master tells you to do." Most slaves found this sort of preaching to be trivial, uninteresting, and offensive.

More appealing were services led by African Americans themselves. Not all slaves had easy access to such services, however. Fearing that slaves might use the time to plan a revolt, many plantation owners did not allow slaves to gather for worship services of their own. Forbidden to meet openly for worship, many slaves held services in secret instead. The possibility of discovery and punishment was always present. But the opportunity to worship as they pleased outweighed the risk.

Quoted in B.A. Botkin, ed., *Lay My Burden Down: A Folk History of Slavery*. Chicago: University of Chicago Press, 1945, p. 25.

of Africa, requiring a reevaluation of where various spirits could be found. And as slaves of differing traditions started to form communities, their religious ideas often began to blend.

Still, traditional African religions could survive and even flourish apart from Africa. Supported by a steady stream of new arrivals from Africa, the slaves of the British colonies continued to worship through the first decades of slavery much as West Africans did. Their connections with traditional African faiths were powerful. One slave remembered his grandfather, a native African, asserting that "the religion of this country [that is, Christianity] was altogether false, and indeed, no religion at all."[4] Until about 1730 and in some cases much longer, this was the prevailing attitude of most slaves, whether born in Africa or merely of African descent.

Christianity

This early focus on traditional African religion was in part the slaves' choice. However, it also had to do with the preferences of the slaveholders. Like the majority of Europeans of the time, nearly all colonial slaveholders were Christians. Though Christians through history have often been eager to convert others to their faith, the British colonists of the 1600s and early 1700s had no interest in introducing Christianity to their slaves. Far from encouraging the slaves to adopt Christian traditions, in fact, they generally tried to keep Christian thought away from the slaves altogether.

In part, this resistance was based on the slaveholders' reading of the Bible. At several points in the Old Testament, God encourages or even commands the Israelites to take slaves for themselves. In these verses, however, God specifies that these slaves must not share the Israelites' religion. "Both thy bondmen, and thy bondmaids, which thou shalt have, shall be of the heathen that are round you," reads Leviticus 25:44. Some white Christians feared that verses such as these obligated them to free any slaves who converted to Christianity. For this reason, it was foolhardy to offer slaves instruction in the Christian faith.

Resistance toward Christianizing the slaves was also rooted in the standard view of race during the time. Most European whites saw blacks as sharply inferior to themselves. White people widely

A white woman reads the Bible to slaves. Initially, many Christians opposed teaching Christianity to black slaves.

believed that Africans and their descendants lacked the intellectual and moral capacity to understand Christianity. In this view, any attempt to help Africans to become Christians would be a waste of effort.

There was a third reason, too, why many masters were eager to keep their slaves from learning about Christianity. That had to do with a basic message of the Christian faith: that God loves all his people equally. Some slaveholders found this message entirely too radical to offer to slaves. If all were equal in the eyes of God, then slaves might question their bondage and demand equality on earth as well. That, whites feared, could lead to outright rebellion. As a group of ministers in South Carolina put it in 1713, "A Slave grows worse by being a Christian."[5]

"Servants, Be Obedient"

But around 1730, these attitudes started to change. Colonists began to reject the notion that newly-converted slaves would need to be released from bondage. Christian leaders revisited the Biblical passages that seemed to forbid Christians from owning other Christians, and concluded that the impact of these verses had been exaggerated. In God's eyes, they said, enslaving blacks of any religion was acceptable. The legal system soon reflected this interpretation, as colonial governments passed laws stating that Christian slaves had no automatic right to freedom. One barrier to the Christianization of slaves had fallen.

At the same time, the white colonists also changed their view of Christianity's effect on slaves. Colonial thinkers now dismissed the idea that a Christian slave would necessarily be an angry slave. Instead, they pointed to Biblical passages urging slaves to be contented with their fate, chief among them the Apostle Paul's command "Servants, be obedient to them that are your masters" (Ephesians 6:5). White colonists argued that verses such as these could convince slaves that their bondage was just and proper. In this way, the introduction of Christianity would calm the slaves and discourage rebellion. As a writer of the time put it "Christianity has a tendency to tame fierce and wild tempers."[6]

Also important was the Great Awakening, a series of religious revivals that swept across white America in the 1730s and beyond. The revivalists, or evangelicals, who led the movement made it their mission to convert as many people to Christianity as possible. They preached tirelessly to anyone who would listen, regardless of education, social status, or even race. "All classes of society were welcome to participate actively in prayer meetings and revival services," writes historian Albert Raboteau. "The poor, the illiterate, and even the enslaved were permitted to preach and pray in public."[7]

"There Are Multitudes of Them"

By the 1730s, moreover, many African Americans were ready to hear the Christian message. Slavery had changed significantly in the previous century. Increasingly, slaves in the colonies had been born in North America. They no longer spoke African languages or had any direct memory of Africa. At the same time, most slaves lived on small farms in close proximity to whites and often at a distance from most other blacks. Without a critical mass of slaves to carry on African religious traditions, the vitality of African faiths was beginning to dwindle.

Beginning in the 1730s, then, slaves across the colonies began to adopt the Christian ideas of the white majority. The process, to be sure, moved slowly and haphazardly. Some African Americans rejected Christianity altogether, reasoning that since it was the religion of their oppressors, it had little to offer the slaves. Other slaves belonged to owners who saw religious instruction and worship as a waste of valuable working hours. One authority suggests that the Christianization of the slaves was not complete even as late as 1820.

But even if not all slaves were Christians, it is clear that Christianity became the dominant faith among American slaves long before 1800. And African Americans who adopted Christianity usually did so with great enthusiasm. "There are multitudes of them," wrote one colonial preacher of the slaves he encountered, "who are willing, and even eagerly desirous to be instructed, and to embrace every opportunity for that end."[8] From the mid-1700s on, the story of slave religion is the story of slave Christianity.

"I Know It Means the Poor African"

In some important ways, the religion of the slaves resembled the religion of the masters. Both slaves and masters typically viewed themselves not merely as Christians but as Protestants—a branch

The Case Against Slavery

Though the Bible was often used by white Southerners to jus-
tify owning slaves, some nineteenth-century thinkers used
biblical texts to argue precisely the opposite. Antislavery activist Lydia Maria Child, for example, had this to say in 1836:

Among other apologies for slavery, it has been asserted
that the Bible does not forbid it. Neither does it forbid
the counterfeiting of a bank-bill. It is the *spirit* of the
Holy Word, not its particular *expressions*, which must
be a rule for our conduct. How can slavery be recon-
ciled with the maxim, "Do unto others, as ye would
that others should do unto you?" Does not the command, "Thou shalt not *steal*," prohibit *kidnapping*?
And how does whipping men to death agree with the
injunction, "Thou shalt do no *murder*?" Are we not
told "to loose the bands of wickedness, to undo the
heavy burdens, to let the oppressed go free, and to
break every yoke?"

Lydia Maria Child, *An Appeal in Favor of That Class of Americans Called Africans*, 1836; repr., New
York: Arno, 1968, p. 32.

of Christianity that rose and flourished in England and other
northern European countries. Slaves and masters each believed
in a single creator God whose son Jesus had suffered and died to
redeem the sins of humanity. Each group accepted the authority
of the Bible in religious matters. Each believed in the power of
prayer. And each looked to ministers to instruct, to preach, and
to interpret the word of God.

At the same time, Christianity as practiced by the slaves did
not always mirror Christianity as practiced by white Americans.
Some of these differences had to do with the emphasis placed on
certain portions of the Bible. African Americans were especially
drawn, for example, to the Old Testament book of Exodus, which
tells of the enslavement of the Hebrews and their eventual escape
from bondage under the leadership of Moses. The slaves saw

Black slaves were drawn to the Old Testament story of the Exodus, which told of Moses and the Israelites crossing the Red Sea.

their own struggles reflected in the oppression of the Hebrews, and they found sustenance in the image of Moses leading his people toward the Promised Land. The story offered African Americans hope that God would similarly bring them out of slavery. "When I heard of [God] delivering his people from bondage," reported one slave, "I know it means the poor African."[9]

The role of emotion was another difference between black and white worship. The open expression of feelings played a vital role in black services. In contrast to white worship services, which could often be staid and formal, the services led and attended by blacks were exciting and unrestrained. "The Negroes sobbed and shouted and swayed backward and forward," reported Mary Chesnut, a white woman who observed a slave service during the 1800s, "most of them clapping their hands and responding in shrill tones: 'Yes, God!' 'Jesus!' 'Savior!' "Bless de Lord, amen,' etc."[10] For most slaves worship was less about engaging the brain than about engaging the heart.

As Chesnut's description indicates, movement and dance were important features of early African American religious expression. Certainly, motion was much more important for the slaves than it was for most white Protestants. Many slaves felt that God compelled them to express their religious devotion through movement. Most could not imagine worshipping in silence and without activity. "You see," one slave argued, "'ligion needs a little motion—specially if you gwine feel de spirret."[11]

"Everywhere, I Prayed"

Another distinction between Christianity as practiced by slaves and Christianity as practiced by white Americans had to do with images of God and Jesus. With some exceptions, especially among the lower classes, white Christians in the early United States tended to view God as removed and somewhat forbidding. Blacks, in contrast, usually felt a strong personal connection with the divine. To them, God was more than a creator staring down at his handiwork from a distance. In the same way, Jesus was a friend and a constant companion as well as being a savior.

This personal connection meant that religion permeated every aspect of slave life. For many slaves religion was not simply an activity to be engaged in once in a while and then ignored until the following week. On the contrary, each part of a slave's day, from eating to working to leisure time, provided an opportunity to connect with God. Often, this took the form of a request that God share the burden of a difficult life. "Everywhere, I prayed," recalled Harriet Tubman, an escaped slave who helped lead many fellow slaves to freedom in the years before the Civil War, "and I groaned to the Lord."[12]

Yet the relationship between God and the slaves was by no means only about complaint. The slaves credited God for all that was good, too—for friends and family, for occasional days of leisure, and most of all for the uncompromising love and acceptance that God alone could offer. In return, the slaves thanked and praised God at every opportunity. Slave worship, as Mary Chesnut noted, echoed with shouts of "Hallelujah!" and "Praise Jesus!" And slaves took comfort in the notion that God would eventually respond to their needs. "I tells 'em, iffen they keeps praying," remarked one slave preacher, "the Lord will set 'em free."[13]

A Blend of Faiths

By the time of the Civil War, Christianity had clearly become the religion of the slaves. With Africa a distant memory at best, American slaves worshipped the Christian god, not the Yoruba deity Olorun; they put their primary trust in Jesus, not in the spirits of their ancestors; and they used English, not Ibo or another tribal language, to call upon God for assistance. The religions of West Africa had seemingly fallen by the wayside.

The truth, however, was more complex. In fact, West African religious thought never entirely disappeared during the years of American slavery. Many features of slave Christianity sprang originally from West African traditional faiths. Just as the slaves emphasized movement in worship, for example, so too did their ancestors. The interjections of "Hallelujah!" and "Bless the Lord!," so common in slave services, had their roots in African call-and-response forms of worship. And the slaves' personal relationship with God and with Jesus was a short step from the West African worldview, in which spirits of ancestors helped guide each individual.

Moreover, Christianity coexisted with beliefs in African-style magic, spirits, and the supernatural. Magicians known as conjurors or "hoodoo doctors," for instance, practiced their craft on many Southern plantations. Many slaves used their services to cast spells on enemies or to remove spells they believed had been cast against them. By the time of the Civil War, the spells no longer bore much resemblance to those used in Africa. Still, the African origin of these spells is clear.

Because these practices did not jibe with mainstream Christian thought, white Americans sometimes questioned the true depth of Christian feelings among the slaves. The slaves, however, strenuously resisted the notion that they were not good Christians merely because they engaged in spells and believed in magic. In their eyes, these practices were simply a part of Christian expression. A slave named George White, for example, once boasted that he could "cure most anything" with his knowledge

Nat Turner

Nat Turner was a slave from Virginia. Intelligent and literate, he felt a particularly close connection with God. He preached frequently to other slaves and was known to many of his fellow workers as "the Prophet."

Turner's experience of Christianity, however, was not orthodox. As a young man he had a series of visions that he interpreted as a call to stage a rebellion. "I heard a loud noise in the heavens," Turner recalled, describing one of these visions, "and the Spirit instantly appeared to me and said the Serpent was loosened, and Christ had laid down the yoke he had borne for the sins of men, and that I should take it on and fight against the Serpent."

In August 1831 Turner and other slaves attacked and killed fifty-five white people. When authorities discovered what was happening, Turner headed into nearby swamps, where he hid for about two months until being captured and executed. While even antislavery activists condemned Turner's actions at the time, several modern African American thinkers have adopted a different perspective. In their eyes Turner was a man of God who was responding the only way he knew how to the evils of slavery.

Quoted in PBS, "Nat Turner's Rebellion," *Africans in America*. www.pbs.org/wgbh/aia/part3/3 p1518.html.

Nat Turner is captured.

African Americans meet outdoors for a prayer meeting.

of magic. In the next breath, however, White noted that magic did not stand alone and could not work without the proper prayers. "You have got to talk wid God," he advised his listeners, "an' ask him to help out."[14]

The Christianity of the slaves, then, owed much to traditional African faiths. By blending African religious ideas with mainstream Christian thought, the slaves developed a form of religious expression that was all their own: a type of Christianity that reflected the needs and the longings of the earliest African Americans. Slave Christianity formed the foundation of the African American religious traditions that would follow.

Chapter Two

The Rise of the Black Church

For generations, many African American Christians have attended so-called "black churches"—churches run by and attended largely, if not exclusively, by African Americans. These churches are religious institutions, of course, but they are often much more than places of worship. In the tiniest southern towns and the largest northern cities, black churches have served as community centers and social welfare organizations, and their ministers have used their positions to speak out on issues of theology, politics, morality, and race. As African American pastor and historian Dwight Perry notes, "The entity at the heart of the Black community in America is the Black church."[13]

Many important influences have helped to shape the modern black church. Three long-term events, however, stand out. The first, which took place in the North in the early years of the United States, was the founding of the black church as an institution. The second was the spread of the black church across the rural South during the period following the Civil War. And the third encompassed the rise of large urban churches at the beginning of the twentieth century. Together, these three stages shaped the black church as a powerful and essential institution.

"They Were No More Plagued by Us"

The black church got its start in the North in the late 1700s. At the time racism was prevalent throughout the United States, and it was as evident in religion as anywhere else. Few Christian denominations allowed African Americans to become full members. Fewer still allowed blacks to preach to mixed-race gatherings or to join church governing bodies. Even in the North, where nearly all blacks were free, many churches discouraged blacks from attending altogether.

One of the more progressive northern churches of the time was St. George Methodist Church in Philadelphia. Unlike many other churches, St. George did have a significant number of blacks in its congregation. St. George also offered occasional services designed specifically for African Americans, many of them led by a black preacher named Richard Allen. Moreover, St. George did not have restricted seating for blacks as other northern churches often did.

The Reverend Richard Allen preached to the black congregation of St. George Methodist Church.

But St. George's relative tolerance did not last. About 1790—accounts differ as to the exact year—a group of blacks that included Allen and a man named Absalom Jones arrived at the church for a regular Sunday service. They were told that they could not take their accustomed seats on the main level of the church. The officials of St. George's had decided to segregate the seating in the building and force blacks to sit in the balcony instead.

Not wishing to disrupt the service by complaining, Allen, Jones, and the others moved up to the second level. But as members of the group knelt in prayer, one church official hurried over. He seized Jones and tried to move him further to the rear of the balcony. Affronted, Jones asked the man to wait till the prayers were over, but the official simply summoned another man to help him. This incident was too much for the African Americans to bear. "We all went out of the church in a body," Allen reported later, "and they were no more plagued by us in the church."[16]

These events had a galvanizing effect on Philadelphia's blacks. If they were unwanted by the city's established churches, they reasoned, then they would simply have to build their own. Allen, Jones, and others tirelessly solicited donations in both the white and black communities of Philadelphia. In the meantime Allen preached on Sundays in a rented storeroom. Little by little the funds for a building grew. In the summer of 1794 the so-called African Church opened its doors for the first time.

St. Thomas and Bethel

Leaders of the new congregation soon voted to associate with the Episcopal Church, which they perceived as more tolerant than the Methodists where racial matters were concerned. Absalom Jones was put in charge of the now-renamed St. Thomas Church. Jones lacked the education expected of Episcopal clergy at the time, but he was respected as a "man of good report and Godly conversation."[17] The church grew quickly, reaching a membership of over four hundred within a year of its founding.

Not all Philadelphia blacks were drawn to St. Thomas, however. Episcopal services tended to be more reserved than those of the Methodists or Baptists, and some local African Americans yearned for worship that might more fully engage their emotions. That was particularly true of Richard Allen. Despite the indignities he had

Reverend Allen founded the Bethel Church for Philadelphia's black population.

suffered at St. George, Allen remained a Methodist at heart. "No religious sect or denomination," he wrote once, "would suit the capacity of the colored people as well as the Methodist."[18]

Allen soon founded Bethel Church, an all-black Philadelphia congregation affiliated with the Methodists. Both St. Thomas and Bethel offered more than worship services. Each, for instance, established and ran a school for African American children. Both churches helped needy African Americans. And both urged local blacks to take pride in themselves despite the racism that pervaded the United States. "We are now encouraged to . . . arise out of the dust and shake ourselves," wrote the leaders of St. Thomas, "and throw off that servile fear, that the habit of oppression and bondage trained us up in."[19]

The AME Church

Neither St. Thomas nor Bethel, however, was truly independent. Although each chose its own leaders, both were still subject to the dictates of their national churches—institutions run entirely by whites. Some leaders of the national Methodist Church, in particular, seemed eager to destroy Allen's congregation. At one point Allen had to convince a court that Bethel's property belonged to the congregation and not to the national church.

Before long, several all-black Methodist congregations were established in northern urban areas, most patterned on Bethel—and most experiencing similar problems. In 1816 Allen and leaders from some of these churches took a major step. Abandoning the national Methodist Church altogether, they formed an entirely new church organization: the African Methodist Episcopal Church, known informally as AME. This was an all-black organization: founded by blacks, run by blacks, and accountable to no one but blacks. For the first time, African Americans had full responsibility for their churches, congregations, and communities.

The AME Church was vital and influential. Between the 1810s and the 1850s the AME Church gained steadily in prominence and numbers throughout the North. In one five year period alone, AME workers helped to establish seventy-two new congregations. The growth of the AME Church also sparked the development of other black church organizations. The AME Zion Church, which broke off

The Bethel AME Church was the first Methodist Church for African Americans in Philadelphia.

from the AME Church in 1821, included dozens of congregations by the time of the Civil War. Similarly, many black Baptist churches sprang up in northern cities and towns during these years.

Black Churches in the North

Like Bethel and St. Thomas, these churches offered blacks a spiritual home—and filled secular needs as well. Many congregations helped destitute blacks, for example. This assistance was based in part on biblical passages that urge Christians to assist the needy, but it was also based on the reality of life in the United States. At the time, government did little to help the poor, and white institutions generally ignored poverty among African Americans. Thus, black churches often filled the gap by providing food, shelter, and clothing to those who lacked them.

Education was an important part of the work of black churches, too. Most free blacks of the nineteenth century were illiterate, and children rarely had much schooling. To many, education seemed to be the path toward a better life. "The church leaders were not educated people," writes a historian, "but they had a clear perception of what education would mean."[20] Thus, church leaders urged congregations to set up classes for both children and adults, and many did just that. These efforts bore particular fruit in 1856, when the AME Church founded Wilberforce University in Ohio, the nation's first college for blacks.

Northern black churches also focused on racial pride and political action. Many pastors, for example, advocated full citizenship rights for free blacks, who were often excluded from the political process. In 1830 several black Methodists called on free blacks to "pursue all legal means for the speedy elevation of ourselves and brethren to the scale and standing of men."[21] African American church members also spoke out against slavery. Many provided a forum for antislavery activists to preach against the slave system. And escaping slaves often made their way to northern black churches, where they were welcomed and given support.

Moving South

Though black churches had a strong impact on African Americans in the pre–Civil War North, they initially had a minimal effect on blacks in the South. When blacks tried to form congregations in

First African Baptist Church

The free African Americans of the North were most responsible for developing the black church as an institution. There were, however, occasional all-black congregations in the pre–Civil War South. In 1777, for example, a group of African Americans led by a former slave named George Liele founded the First African Baptist Church in Savannah, Georgia. Liele, an ordained minister, served as the pastor of the church.

For political reasons, First African Baptist did not remain in existence for long. Liele strongly supported the British side during the American Revolution. When the British were forced to leave Savannah, American officials punished Liele and many of his followers. Liele was briefly put in jail and was  almost returned to slavery; in the end he immigrated to Jamaica. Other members of his congregation were also jailed or forced to leave the country. As a result, the church did not survive. Still, First African Baptist had demonstrated that independent black churches could succeed in the South.

The modern First American Baptist church in Savannah, Georgia, is a descendant of the congregation of 1777.

the South, they usually found themselves blocked by southern whites who distrusted the political messages of northern black churches. But when the Civil War came to an end in 1865, churches began appearing all over the rural South. Hundreds of thousands of the former slaves joined the AME Church, the AME Zion Church, or any of an assortment of Baptist congregations. The second stage of the black church had begun.

The success of African American churches in the South relied on several factors. One was simply the religious message they offered. Many of the former slaves had lived on plantations where religious expression was discouraged or where all services were designed and led by whites. The idea of an independent black church was strongly appealing to these men and women, and many observers commented on the zeal with which southern blacks approached the Gospel. "Every word you say while preaching, they drink down and respond to, with an earnestness that sets your heart all on fire,"[22] wrote AME official James Lynch about African Americans in South Carolina.

Black churches were also effective in the South because they relied on blacks for leadership. During slavery, of course, African Americans had little opportunity to create community institutions of their own. Following the Civil War, southern whites continued to dominate most aspects of society: They led state and local governments, they ran the schools, and they organized the economy. Only

Independent African American churches such as this one appealed to southern blacks.

the black church allowed African Americans to guide and to govern. As Perry points out, "The historic Black church was the first institution, and for two hundred or more years the only institution, led and controlled by African Americans."[23]

And black churches were successful across the South, finally, because they were urgently needed. The Civil War had given southern slaves little more than their freedom. The overwhelming majority of southern blacks were uneducated, powerless, and desperately poor. The federal government and some white churches offered help for a few years following the Civil War, but it soon became clear to most southern blacks that they could not expect much from white-dominated institutions. Black churches were the only real alternative.

Roles of the Church

Like their counterparts in the North, southern blacks turned their new churches into focal points of their communities. Many of the church buildings were little more than shacks, and few congregations had much money; still, whatever the former slaves needed, the black churches of the South sought to provide. Sometimes that was education. In Savannah, Georgia, black churches established ten schools before the Civil War officially came to an end. Southern churches also provided economic help; many formed mutual aid societies, in which members pooled some of their resources to assist those in need.

Most black preachers in the South also discussed racial issues. They urged their congregations not to lose faith because of the bitter discrimination around them. Some of these preachers reminded southern blacks that heaven would be a better place; others emphasized the hope of creating a more just society in the present world. And a few preachers advocated a thorough restructuring of the way many African Americans thought about race. Rather than being ashamed of their skin color, these preachers believed, blacks should celebrate themselves. "Why should not the Negro believe that he resembles God as much so as other people?"[24] asked Georgia minister Henry Taylor.

Black churches in the South took on other responsibilities, too. Some Baptist and Methodist organizations published newsletters and religious materials. Several churches formed missionary groups to spread Christianity through Africa; as one Baptist minister put it, "God's purpose is to redeem Africa through us."[25] Others sponsored singing groups or other clubs, providing social opportunities for members. And still others helped to found black business associations.

Some of this work had been done in the North as well. The realities of life in the South, though, meant that these projects often had a different meaning for southern black churches. Mutual aid societies were a good example. Though familiar to northerners—Allen and Jones had helped found one in Philadelphia—they took on new importance in southern black churches. Recognizing that southern blacks had few if any reliable sources of credit, southern churches not only set up mutual aid societies but helped to establish banks and insurance companies as well.

And of course, the effects of southern black churches were much more substantial. That was because the great bulk of nineteenth-century African Americans lived in the South. For all the northern black churches had done, they had been able to help only a small proportion of African Americans. The work of southern black churches reached far more people—and had, therefore, a much wider impact.

The Great Migration

The black church had grown considerably during its move south. In the process it had responded to new challenges and realities without losing sight of its fundamental mission and responsibility. It had demonstrated that it appealed equally well to small groups of urban northerners as to the great masses of African Americans in the rural South. But by the early twentieth century, further changes were on the way. Forced to adapt once again, the black church began the third stage of its development—a stage that brought it back to its urban roots.

This time, the black church was forced to respond to population shifts. Fed up with poverty and racial prejudice, rural southern blacks began leaving their farms in the years before World War I. "They moved because the sheriff was mean, because planters were mean, because life was mean,"[26] says one historian. Some moved to urban areas elsewhere in the South, such as Memphis and Atlanta. The great majority, however, moved north

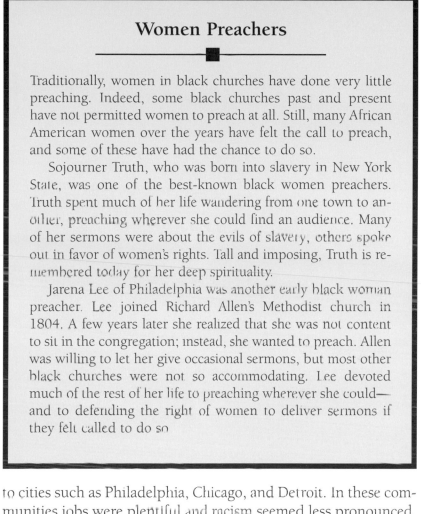

Women Preachers

Traditionally, women in black churches have done very little preaching. Indeed, some black churches past and present have not permitted women to preach at all. Still, many African American women over the years have felt the call to preach, and some of these have had the chance to do so.

Sojourner Truth, who was born into slavery in New York State, was one of the best-known black women preachers. Truth spent much of her life wandering from one town to another, preaching wherever she could find an audience. Many of her sermons were about the evils of slavery, others spoke out in favor of women's rights. Tall and imposing, Truth is remembered today for her deep spirituality.

Jarena Lee of Philadelphia was another early black woman preacher. Lee joined Richard Allen's Methodist church in 1804. A few years later she realized that she was not content to sit in the congregation; instead, she wanted to preach. Allen was willing to let her give occasional sermons, but most other black churches were not so accommodating. Lee devoted much of the rest of her life to preaching wherever she could— and to defending the right of women to deliver sermons if they felt called to do so

to cities such as Philadelphia, Chicago, and Detroit. In these communities jobs were plentiful and racism seemed less pronounced. By 1930 hundreds of thousands of blacks had made their way north—so many, in fact, that the process became known as the Great Migration.

Life in the cities, however, presented new problems. Though many African Americans did find jobs as factory workers or domestic servants, their pay was low and their work hours long. Accustomed to farming, many of these new arrivals had trouble adjusting to the pace of urban life, and African Americans routinely faced discrimination in housing. To make matters worse, many blacks had left behind friends and family members who had provided support in the rural South. And no white-run institution in

Black women weigh wire coils and record weights in this 1919 photo.

the cities seemed eager to smooth the way for the people of the Great Migration.

Once again the black church stepped forward. Existing urban churches added space, staff, and services to meet the needs of the new arrivals. Some embarked on building projects that doubled or tripled the size of the original church. The extra space was sorely needed. "The people are coming from the south every week," a young woman from Akron, Ohio, wrote in 1917. "The Baptist Church is over crowded with Baptist[s] from Ala & Ga [Alabama and Georgia]. 10 [or] 12 join every Sunday."[27]

But churches could not build quickly enough to accommodate the growing population. Some of the migrants, too, were eager to replicate the smaller rural churches in their home states. Thus, blacks in the North often formed new churches and opened them in whatever space they could find. Quite often, these spaces were in commercial districts and did not resemble traditional churches at all. "The rural Black church," Dwight Perry observes, "became an urban storefront."[28]

What mattered, though, was not the beauty of the church building but what went on inside it, and for the most part black churches were able to meet the needs of the new arrivals. The worship experience was a major part of those needs. In the early

The Abyssinian Baptist Church located in Harlem in New York City, became known for its soup kitchens.

1900s traditional Methodist and Baptist services were joined by a new form of worship known as Pentecostalism. Pentecostal churches were known for emotionally intense services during which the Holy Spirit—one manifestation of the Christian god—was said to be present. "There came a wave of glory into me," said an early Pentecostal about a service, "and all of my being was filled with the glory of the Lord."[29] Pentecostalism added to the breadth of available worship services in the black community.

Once again, though, churches provided more than simply a spiritual experience. As before, black churches offered African

A Black Jesus

In American Christian churches, books, and illustrations, Jesus has usually been portrayed as a white man with pale eyes and light hair. Such depictions have been common in black churches as well as in white ones. For years, however, some African Americans have waged a struggle to rid black churches of these images, which they see as damaging to black Christians.

As early as 1895, for example, Baptist clergyman Henry Turner advocated that blacks should think of both Jesus and God as black. In the 1960s Detroit preacher Albert B. Cleage went even further. "Jesus was a Black Messiah," he argued, "born to a black woman. . . . When I say Jesus was black, I'm not saying, 'Wouldn't it be nice if Jesus was black?' . . . I'm saying that Jesus WAS black. There never was a white Jesus."

Today, some black congregations have followed the lead of Turner and Cleage. A painting at Trinity United Church of Christ in Chicago, for instance, shows a black Jesus beside an African American family. And the Sixteenth Street Baptist Church in Birmingham, Alabama, has a stained glass window that depicts Jesus as black. However, many black Christians, especially those most mindful of tradition, continue to be more comfortable with images of a white Jesus.

Quoted in Mark L. Chapman, *Christianity on Trial.* Maryknoll, NY: Orbis, 1996, pp. 98–99.

Americans positions of leadership. Members who toiled at low-wage, low-status jobs could serve as deacons, Sunday school teachers, or solo musicians; some filled important posts in church government. The ability to lead had been important earlier in the black church, but it became even more important now, with so many African Americans trying to find their way in a strange new place.

And urban black churches, especially the largest ones, became true community centers during this period. Olivet Baptist Church in Chicago, for example, opened a day care center and an employment bureau, in addition to sponsoring sports teams, drama groups, and continuing education classes for adults. Abyssinian Baptist in Harlem, New York, became known for its soup kitchens. New Bethel in Detroit established a variety of self help organizations and even a nursing corps.

Finally, black churches offered people of the Great Migration a valuable link to their former lives. The bustling cities of the North were huge, unfamiliar, and disorienting, but the black churches offered comfort and stability to the new arrivals. Despite new roles and responsibilities, the basic thrust and mission of African American churches remained the same: to care for black people, both in this world and in the next. For the new arrivals the churches were a constant. They provided a tie to the world the people of the Great Migration had once known.

The black church had begun in the urban North and moved to the rural South; now it returned to the northern cities where it had begun. At each point, it remained the most powerful black institution in the United States. Through all three stages, it encouraged, strengthened, and empowered its people. African Americans across the country deeply appreciated the church and all that it offered. As black author Richard Wright once wrote, "It is only when we are within the walls of our churches that we are wholly ourselves."[30]

Chapter Three

Black Sacred Music

Throughout history the African American religious experience has been marked by several distinctive characteristics. For one, African Americans have typically emphasized a personal relationship between themselves and God. For another, black worship has tended to be heavily focused on preaching. And for a third, most African American congregations place great value on emotional services that engage the heart and the spirit as well as the mind.

But of all the characteristics common to black worship, music is perhaps the one most closely identified with African American religious expression. Since the earliest days of American history, music has been a central part of black worship. The musical styles used in African American services have varied considerably, from drumming to gospel and from spirituals to hip-hop. Still, the presence of music has been constant. Innovative and emotional, joyful and despairing, black sacred music has long been at the heart of the black church. As one African American music minister puts it, "Singing is as necessary for worship as breathing is for life."[31]

African Traditions

The story of African American religious music begins with the first blacks to arrive in the British colonies. The people of West Africa were skilled musicians who used chants, dancing, and drums as an essential part of their worship. In Africa, as historians C. Eric Lincoln and Lawrence Mamiya write, "Music and religion and life itself were all one holistic enterprise"[32]—that is, they could not easily be separated. In West African traditional culture, to make music was to worship, and to worship was to make music.

The earliest black Americans were unable to replicate the music of Africa exactly as their ancestors had performed it. Many white masters barred their slaves from drumming, for example, for fear that slaves might revolt by sending coded messages from one farm to another via the drums. Likewise, the specific steps of many dances were gradually lost through time. Nonetheless, the basic vitality and importance of African music remained. And many observers, both white and black, saw clear similarities between the music of Africans and the music of the slaves.

A contemporary African dance troupe keeps African musical traditions alive.

The so-called "ring shout" was an excellent example. This form of worship, which combined music and movement, was popular in slave communities—and in some cases, in the post–Civil War South as well. Black writer and musician James Weldon Johnson described the ring shout as follows:

> "A space is cleared . . . and the men and women arrange themselves, generally alternately, in a ring, their bodies quite close. The music starts and the ring begins to move. Around it goes, at first slowly, then with quickening pace. . . . The music is supplemented by the clapping of hands. As the ring goes around it begins to take on signs of frenzy. . . . The music becomes a wild, monotonous chant. The same musical phrase is repeated over and over one, two, three, four, five hours."[33]

Johnson assumed that the ring shout was "the survival of a primitive African dance,"[34] and modern scholars believe he was correct.

The music of the early slaves was reminiscent of Africa in other ways as well. Though drums were not allowed, slaves often beat out complex rhythms by slapping their hands against their legs. Most of these rhythms were not used in standard European music. Popular slave instruments such as the banjo had their roots in West Africa, too; along with violins and other instruments of European origin, banjos were sometimes used in slave worship.

The style of singing used by many slaves also seemed to have little in common with the music of white Americans. Many white listeners perceived African American vocal techniques as exotic and unfamiliar. Lucy McKim, a nineteenth-century collector of songs, noted that African American vocalists often made use of "odd turns made in the throat" and "slides from one note to another."[35] While they certainly were "odd" to western ears, however, these vocal features are common in the music of West Africans. In all likelihood, then, the musical styles McKim heard had an African origin.

Spirituals

As Christianity became more popular among the slaves, the music used in African American worship changed. By the mid-1700s black Americans had begun to develop a kind of song known today as the spiritual. Spirituals were deeply religious

Sacred Songs and Worldly Meanings

Spirituals and gospel songs were fundamentally about religion, but some had secondary meanings. The spiritual "Steal Away," for instance, spoke of the slaves' longing to "steal away to Jesus, steal away home"—that is, to join Christ for eternity. Yet the song also referenced a more worldly way in which slaves could steal away: by escaping from their masters. There is evidence that some slaves used songs like these to help them communicate escape plans among themselves.

Gospel music often had a double meaning too. On the surface, for instance, the classic song "Move On Up a Little Higher," composed by Memphis minister W.H. Brewster, was strictly about religion. The title and lyrics simply exhorted listeners to reach for heaven. But as Brewster noted in an interview, he was talking about more than just the afterlife: He was also trying to inspire blacks to reach for jobs, education, and other secular pursuits. Like the early spirituals, Brewster's song worked on more than one level.

Quoted in James Weldon Johnson and J. Rosamond Johnson, *The Books of American Negro Spirituals.* New York: Viking, 1940, p. 114.

songs based on Christian themes and images, many taken directly from the stories of the Bible. Some of the spirituals of the pre–Civil War era are still well known today; among the most familiar are "Deep River," "Go Down, Moses," and "Swing Low, Sweet Chariot."

Spirituals varied considerably. Some were slow and introspective and spoke to the longing of the slaves for a better world. Often, these were known as "sorrow songs." "Nobody knows de trouble I've seen," ran the first line of one popular sorrow song, "nobody knows but Jesus."[36] Other spirituals, however, were meant to be sung at a much faster tempo. These were joyful songs of praise and celebration, which glorified God and spoke of the promise of a better future. As one of these livelier songs put it:

"I got a robe, you got a robe,
All o' God's chillun got robes.
When I get to heab'n I'm goin' to put on my robe,
I'm goin' to shout all ovah God's Heav'n."[37]

Regardless of the tempo of a spiritual, most of these songs reminded the slaves that there was hope, whether in this world or the next, and that one way or another, black Americans would eventually be free. Many spirituals expressed the deep connection slaves often felt with Jesus. Other stories and images commonly found in spirituals included the escape of the Hebrew slaves from Egypt, the sufferings of Jesus on the cross, and the promised Day of Judgment, when good would triumph over evil. One well-known spiritual, for example, looked forward to the day when God would "take de righteous home to glory" to "live wid God forever."[38]

Slaves on a southern plantation keep hope alive by singing spirituals and other songs.

Because they spoke so clearly to the slaves' experiences, spirituals made up an important part of slave worship—and an important part of slave life in general. Visitors to the pre–Civil War South often reported hearing slaves sing spirituals as they worked in the fields, and many former slaves recalled singing them at informal gatherings, too. Spirituals, indeed, were a community experience. When they were being sung, all blacks present were expected to take part to the best of their abilities. "If a member of the group could not sing," notes a historian, "he could tap his foot; if he could not tap, he could sway his head, and if he could not do this, he could witness."[39]

European Hymns

Spirituals remained popular among African Americans throughout the years of slavery. Following the Civil War, though, they began to fall out of favor. To many blacks, spirituals became an uncomfortable reminder of the slave system. These African Americans wanted new musical forms and methods of expression instead. To fill this need, they often looked to nearby white churches for inspiration. Many of these churches had a rich tradition of singing hymns, notably hymns created during the 1700s by an Englishman named Isaac Watts, and quite a few black churches eagerly adopted these hymns as their own.

Black Christians, however, did not sing these hymns quite the way white Christians did. In black churches hymns were frequently sung using a process known as hymn-lining. In hymn-lining, a preacher, deacon, or other music minister sang the first line of the hymn; then the congregation sang it back. The leader continued in this way, line by line, until the entire hymn had been sung. Hymn lining made good sense for the freed slaves. Poor and largely illiterate, they could not have made much use of hymnals even if they had been able to afford them.

Conventional English hymns were transformed in other ways by African American singers, too. African American Baptists, in particular, altered the music significantly; some scholars say that the Baptists "blackened" the hymns. Black congregations changed the hymns' time signatures and rhythms, and they sometimes changed the melodies. Moreover, they made frequent use of improvisation—that is, making up new words or music on the spot.

These "blackened" hymns are still an important part of music in many black churches.

Gospel Music

During the late nineteenth century another musical form began to appear in African American churches. This new style was known as gospel music. The word *gospel* means "good news," and the purpose of gospel music was to spread the "good news" of Jesus Christ. Accordingly, gospel songs told of the mighty power and love of God and emphasized the great joys that awaited Christians in heaven. More even than spirituals, gospel music celebrated the close relationship between God and his people. God "will take away each sorrow," ran the lyrics to a typical gospel song, "Let Him have your burdens now."[40]

Musically, gospel songs were different from earlier hymns and spirituals. Though some early gospel songs were set to music that

The Harlem Gospel Choir performs in 2006. Gospel music was different from earlier hymns and spirituals.

called to mind standard European hymns, most gospel music was not at all traditional. Instead, these songs used elements of jazz and the blues, two secular styles then developing among African Americans in the South and elsewhere. Like these new forms, gospel was characterized in part by strong yet flexible rhythms, intricate accompaniments, and improvisation.

But gospel songs were more than their melodies, and more even than their lyrics. For most gospel singers, gospel was foremost a deeply emotional response to God. The specifics of words, tune, and singer were not so important as the spirit with which the music was sung. "It ain't the voice," says one gospel singer. "Sometimes somebody with the squeakiest voice can say what we want to hear."[41] The fundamental appeal of gospel, then, was to the emotions and the soul, not to the head or the intellect. The purpose of gospel music was to fill listeners with a sense of the divine.

Easing the Pain

Just as spirituals stemmed from the experience of slavery, so too was gospel music sparked by the realities of African American life: in this case, the Great Migration. Many gospel songs were a direct response to the difficult conditions of life in the urban North. Separated from friends and family and discriminated against in jobs, schools, and housing, most African Americans longed to hear a positive message. "Gospel music," writes Perry, "arrived on the scene just in time to ease the pain a little."[42]

Indeed, many of the earliest gospel composers and musicians were southerners who had moved north. Born in slave territory in Maryland, C.A. Tindley was living in Philadelphia when he began writing gospel songs in 1900. Tindley is perhaps best known today for his 1916 song, "I'll Overcome Someday," which eventually became the civil rights song "We Shall Overcome." Thomas Dorsey, also a southerner by birth, rose to prominence for his gospel music while living in Chicago during the 1920s and 1930s. Dorsey's best-known compositions include "Take My Hand, Precious Lord" and "Peace in the Valley."

But though gospel spoke to the experiences of urban African Americans, it struggled to catch on at first. African American church members who valued tradition often found the new

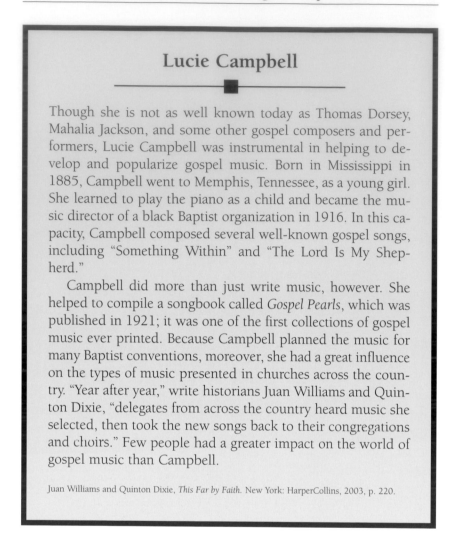

Lucie Campbell

Though she is not as well known today as Thomas Dorsey, Mahalia Jackson, and some other gospel composers and performers, Lucie Campbell was instrumental in helping to develop and popularize gospel music. Born in Mississippi in 1885, Campbell went to Memphis, Tennessee, as a young girl. She learned to play the piano as a child and became the music director of a black Baptist organization in 1916. In this capacity, Campbell composed several well-known gospel songs, including "Something Within" and "The Lord Is My Shepherd."

Campbell did more than just write music, however. She helped to compile a songbook called *Gospel Pearls*, which was published in 1921; it was one of the first collections of gospel music ever printed. Because Campbell planned the music for many Baptist conventions, moreover, she had a great influence on the types of music presented in churches across the country. "Year after year," write historians Juan Williams and Quinton Dixie, "delegates from across the country heard music she selected, then took the new songs back to their congregations and choirs." Few people had a greater impact on the world of gospel music than Campbell.

Juan Williams and Quinton Dixie, *This Far by Faith*. New York: HarperCollins, 2003, p. 220.

music distasteful. Some preferred their songs to be based on biblical themes, which were an important part of hymns and spirituals but were much less frequent in gospel. More significantly, gospel's relationship to the secular musical forms of jazz and the blues was suspect. Some preachers called gospel "sin music" and refused to allow it in their sanctuaries. "I've been thrown out of some of the best churches in America,"[43] Dorsey remarked.

Popularity

But as time went on, gospel began to take hold—in the South as well as in the North. That was particularly true among Pentecostal churches. Since these churches already emphasized emotional responses to God, they were drawn to the passionate gospel style. Mahalia Jackson, who went on to become one of the most celebrated gospel singers in history, grew up in the comparatively staid Baptist Church, but she recalled the excitement of the music she heard during worship at a Pentecostal church near her home in the early 1920s:

> These people had no choir and no organ. They used the drum, the cymbal, the tambourine, and the steel triangle. Everybody in there sang and stomped their feet and sang with their whole bodies. They had a beat, a powerful beat, a rhythm we held on to from slavery days, and their music was so strong and expressive it used to bring tears to my eyes.[44]

The excitement Jackson felt in listening to gospel was contagious. During the 1930s and 1940s gospel became wildly popular. African Americans flocked to churches and concert halls to hear soloists such as Jackson, Marion Williams, and Roberta Martin. Larger gospel groups also made their names during this period and beyond. A male quartet called the Dixie Hummingbirds, for example, brought gospel to eager listeners all over the country.

Mahalia Jackson sings at the New Orleans Jazz Festival on April 23, 1970.

The popularity of gospel was enhanced by the advent of radio and recordings in the early twentieth century. Both brought gospel music even to people in small rural communities. Jackson's 1946 recording of "Move On Up a Little Higher" sold more than 1 million copies, a testament to the power of gospel for its listeners. Improvements in transportation helped, too. As travel became easier, many gospel performers went on tour. Professional singers rented buses and vans and set out to visit dozens of churches on what became known as the "gospel highway."[45] The effect, again, was to spread the gospel message to a greater audience.

The performance of gospel music by solo acts and small groups made sense. Because gospel was heavily improvisational, it did not always lend itself to congregational singing. Instead, it was often easier for churches to have soloists or a well-rehearsed ensemble

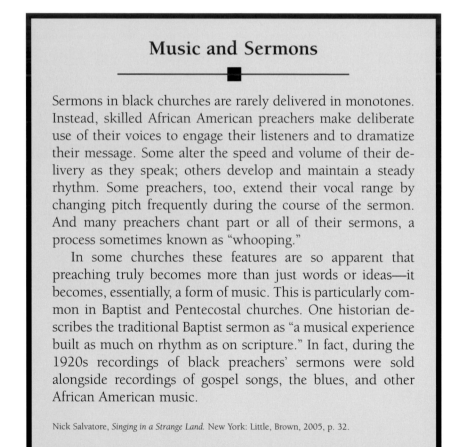

Music and Sermons

Sermons in black churches are rarely delivered in monotones. Instead, skilled African American preachers make deliberate use of their voices to engage their listeners and to dramatize their message. Some alter the speed and volume of their delivery as they speak; others develop and maintain a steady rhythm. Some preachers, too, extend their vocal range by changing pitch frequently during the course of the sermon. And many preachers chant part or all of their sermons, a process sometimes known as "whooping."

In some churches these features are so apparent that preaching truly becomes more than just words or ideas—it becomes, essentially, a form of music. This is particularly common in Baptist and Pentecostal churches. One historian describes the traditional Baptist sermon as "a musical experience built as much on rhythm as on scripture." In fact, during the 1920s recordings of black preachers' sermons were sold alongside recordings of gospel songs, the blues, and other African American music.

Nick Salvatore, *Singing in a Strange Land.* New York: Little, Brown, 2005, p. 32.

serve as song leaders instead of having all church members sing. When the lead singers were truly filled with the spirit, they produced music that electrified their audiences. Swept up by the excitement created by soloists or quartets, members of the congregation often joined in with handclapping and cries of "Amen!"

At the same time, though, the emphasis on performance represented a change in the way black churches viewed music. Where ordinary church members had once been encouraged to join in the singing of hymns or spirituals, now they were more commonly treated as an audience. They were, certainly, a deeply involved audience, whose responses to the singers were welcomed and included as part of the worship experience; still, they were spectators more than actual participants. In this way, the trend toward gospel limited the ability of ordinary churchgoers to make their own music during worship.

African American Music Today

Today, gospel remains a living force in African American music. Many gospel songs from the early twentieth century are still widely sung today, and new gospel pieces continue to be written. These newer songs often incorporate rhythms and melodic features that would have been unfamiliar to earlier masters such as Dorsey and Tindley. Even so, the emotional energy of these pieces make them easily recognizable as gospel. "It's [still] the hand-clapping, foot-patting, throw-your-hands-up-in-the-air kind of music my granddaddy taught me as a child,"[46] says gospel performer John P. Kee.

Gospel, however, is not the only musical style popular in modern African American worship. Some older forms of black sacred music are used today, too. Spirituals, once scorned by blacks embarrassed by their history, have made a comeback. At many black churches they are sung frequently—and not as a historical curiosity but as a living way to worship God and to connect with the past. Similarly, some black churches maintain the hymn-lining tradition of the nineteenth century, and many more continue to use traditional English hymns as an important part of their musical offering. Like the spirituals, the hymns of the earlier African American church still speak to black Christians.

At the same time, African American worship is incorporating broader musical styles. The great musician Duke Ellington, for

Duke Ellington performs with his band in New York in 1943.

instance, wrote several sacred jazz pieces for performance in worship settings. A New York State group called the Dance Ministry Institute presents sacred dances based on African and American music and movements. And a few urban Episcopal churches have begun combining Christian worship with hip-hop music. The resulting "hip-hop masses" are featured services in some of these congregations.

Whatever the source and style of music in African American services, music has always been a vital part of black worship. At heart, each genre of music common to the African American church is an offering of love and a reflection of the singer's deepest feelings. As one singer puts it, "I want to lift my voice in praise and thanksgiving for what God has done for me and so many others. . . . I consider it a great privilege to come together with others to sing praise and worship to God."[47]

Chapter Four

African American Islam

Today, the great majority of African Americans identify themselves as Christian. Still, Christianity is not the only religion that attracts American blacks. Well-known blacks who have converted to Buddhism for example include singer Tina Turner and writer Alice Walker. Some scholars estimate that perhaps fifty thousand American Jews are black. And a few African Americans belong to African-derived religions such as Santeria, which originated among the slaves of the Caribbean and is still quite popular in places such as Haiti.

The religion that attracts the largest share of non-Christian African Americans, however, is Islam. Population estimates differ, but it seems clear that between 1 and 2 million black Americans are Muslims. Though this number is quite low compared to the number of black Christians, it is growing. In addition, Islam's influence on African America has often gone beyond its relatively small numbers. Politically and spiritually, Islam represents an important part of African American religious expression.

A woman and her daughter wear traditional Islamic head scarves in Harlem.

Muslim Slaves

Islam developed in the Middle East in the 600s and spread west-ward into Africa during the medieval period. By 1100 Islam had become the leading religion across much of the Sahara Desert. Over the next few centuries Islam moved south into the West African forests and made its way toward Africa's well-populated Atlantic coastline. Though Islam never came to dominate these regions as it had in the desert, it was nonetheless well received by many West Africans and became the chosen religion of several West African peoples.

The spread of Islam meant that at least some of the African slaves obtained by European traders and sea captains were Mus-lims. By some estimates, Islam was the faith of perhaps 10 per-cent of the slaves brought to North America. Whites occasionally took notice of the Muslims among them, noting from time to time that one or more of their new purchases maintained Muslim tra-ditions. Similarly, a handful of literate Muslim slaves mentioned their religion in written documents. "Before I came to the Chris-tian country," wrote North Carolina slave Omar ibn Said in 1831, "my religion was the religion of Mohammed [Muhammad], the Apostle of God."[48]

But Islamic beliefs and practices did not linger in North Amer-ica for long. One reason was that American slaves most often lived in small, isolated communities rather than on large planta-tions. As a result, many Muslim slaves lived far from anyone who shared their religion. Even the children of Muslims generally had a non-Muslim parent. Without a significant number of Muslim slaves who could pass on traditions and stories, Islam soon began to disappear among African Americans.

Then again, Islam did not endure even where there were large numbers of Muslims. In Africa the spread of Islam relied heavily on Muslim schools, set up specifically to educate young people in the ways of the religion. Under slavery, however, such schools were impossible to establish. Moreover, Islam relies heavily on printed material, and books and other reading matter were for-bidden to slaves. "Though many Muslims memorize significant sections of their holy text [the Koran]," authors Juan Williams and Quinton Dixie note, "their ability to recall such passages quickly faded without ways to reinforce retention."[49]

Ibrahima Abdul Rahman

One of the most unusual life stories of any North American slave belongs to Ibrahima Abdul Rahman. A literate Muslim who grew up in the West African interior, Abdul Rahman came from a noble background. In 1788, however, he was captured by a rival African group, sold to white traders, and transported to Louisiana, where he was purchased by a plantation owner named Thomas Foster.

Abdul Rahman hoped that his noble background and his literacy might earn him his freedom. Indeed, several local whites encouraged Foster to set him free. But Foster always refused, and year by year Abdul Rahman's dreams dimmed. He eventually married a Christian slave named Isabella, though he kept his own identity as a Muslim.

Then, in 1826 Abdul Rahman asked a local white man, Andrew Marschalk, to help him send a letter to present-day Mali, where Abdul Rahman had grown up. Marschalk agreed, but sent the letter to Morocco instead. It was a fortunate mistake. The Moroccan government took an interest in Abdul Rahman and pressed Foster to release him. Under the circumstances, Foster eventually agreed. Finally free, Abdul Rahman and his wife immigrated to Liberia in West Africa, where he died in 1829.

The result was inevitable. Without copies of the Koran and other holy books, without the ability to set up schools, and without a large centralized population of Muslims, Islam had little chance to flourish in North America. By the time of the Civil War, hardly any American blacks would have considered themselves Muslim. Some historians believe that traces of Islam were incorporated into slave worship, but the religion itself had essentially disappeared.

Noble Drew Ali

Throughout most of the nineteenth century, then, Islam remained more or less unknown to American blacks. In the early 1900s, though, Muslim ideas and principles slowly began making inroads into African American life and culture. The forms of Islam introduced in the United States were different in several important ways from Islam as practiced in Africa and the Middle East. Nonetheless, the African Americans who adopted these ideas considered themselves Muslims, and there is no question that they based their worship heavily on Muslim beliefs and theories.

The first of these Muslim innovators was an African American man named Noble Drew Ali. Born in North Carolina in 1886, Ali was originally given the name Timothy Drew, but changed his name during the early 1900s to reflect a new interest in Islam. Little is known about Ali's early life. As a result, no one can tell where and when Ali first encountered Islamic ideas. Nor is it clear whether he had any formal training in Muslim thought. Some

Black Muslims pray at a mosque in New York.

stories claim that he studied with Muslim scholars in Egypt or Saudi Arabia, but it seems equally possible that he never left the United States.

In 1913, in any case, Ali founded a house of worship in Newark, New Jersey. Known first as the Canaanite Temple and later as the Moorish Science Temple—"Moorish" was a word frequently used to refer to Muslims at the time—the new institution was designed to bring Islam to the African Americans of Newark. In particular, Ali wrote and spoke extensively about Allah, the Muslim name for God. "Allah," he wrote, "is all God, all mercy, and all power; he is perfect and holy, all wisdom, all knowledge, all truth."[50] Ali also taught his followers that Muhammad, who had developed Islam in the 600s, was Allah's great prophet, and he focused on common Muslim concepts such as unity and justice.

Ali identified with Islam in less overtly religious ways as well. For instance, he required his followers to call themselves Moors rather

Santeria

◼

Since the early days of slavery a few African Americans have adhered to Santeria, a faith heavily influenced by traditional African religious ideas. The worship of spirits, for example, is an important part of Santeria. Animal sacrifice, particularly of chickens, is common in Santeria, too, and worship often includes dance and music.

Santeria originated among slaves in the Caribbean. While it did make its way to North America early on, it did not gain much of a foothold in the South. During the 1960s, though, interest in things African began to grow among many black Americans. As blacks adopted African clothing styles, African hairdos, and African names, they sought out African religions as well. As a result, Santeria slowly picked up adherents among American blacks of the time. Today, Santeria remains a minor religion within the United States, but one that is practiced by at least some Americans—both native-born converts and immigrants from the Caribbean.

than Negroes, the standard designation for blacks at the time. He also had them wear distinctive Middle Eastern or Asian headgear such as turbans. Both requirements tended to separate temple members from the bulk of African Americans in the community and mark them as Muslims. Similarly, Ali adopted the flag of Morocco, a heavily Islamic country, as the symbol of his new temple.

Politics and Religion

Despite these obviously Muslim features, Ali's teachings did not always adhere to orthodox Islam. Indeed, a typical African or Middle Eastern Muslim of the time would not have considered the Moorish Science Temple to be truly Muslim. Ali did not counsel his followers to make pilgrimages to the holy city of Mecca in Saudi Arabia, for instance, though making this journey at least once in a lifetime is an obligation for Muslims. Nor did he have members of his temple fast during the month of Ramadan, another requirement for Muslims elsewhere. And unlike Muslim leaders in the rest of the world, Ali rarely provided his followers with standard Islamic literature.

Then again, Ali's message was not simply religious; it was also political. Ali had little trust in the ability and willingness of white people to help African Americans. He advocated instead self-determination and racial pride, and in his eyes, those goals meshed better with Islam than with Christianity. Ali saw Christianity as a white religion with little to offer blacks, while Islam, in contrast, was a non-Western faith with a strong connection to Africa. The emphasis on the Moorish Temple's Islamic features thus served a secular purpose as well as a spiritual one.

At first, Ali's ideas proved quite popular among African Americans. By the mid-1920s Ali had opened temples in cities across the North, and an estimated fifty thousand African Americans had joined the movement. But the Moorish Science Temple did not flourish for long. Arguments within the organization, mismanagement of funds, and the mysterious death of Ali in 1929 damaged and eventually destroyed the organization. Still, the Moorish Science Temple had given black Americans an alternative to Christianity.

The Nation of Islam

The appeal of the Moorish Science Temple among blacks inspired other African Americans to set up similar organizations of their own. The most prominent of these, the Nation of Islam, was established

W. D. Fard established the Nation of Islam.

in Detroit about 1930. The founder of this organization was a black man named W.D. Fard, who also called himself Wali Fard Muhammad. Fard was well positioned to start a new sect. Like Ali, Fard most likely had limited training in Islam, but he worked as a door-to-door salesman in Detroit's African American community—a job that made it easy to spread information about his new religious group.

Theologically, the Nation of Islam picked up most of the ideas of the Moorish Science Temple. Like Ali, Fard incorporated some aspects of mainstream Islam into his new organization. Members of the group were instructed to pray to Allah, for example, and were also told to refrain from eating pork, a food banned throughout the Muslim world. And of course the group's name—the Nation of Islam—indicated Muslim origins.

At the same time, Fard advocated new religious notions of his own, many of which had nothing to do with orthodox Muslim thought. His thinking was influenced by sources as varied as Baptist radio preachers and the Freemasons—a fraternal organization of long standing known for its religious overtones. Like Ali, Fard ignored or rejected many standard Muslim requirements. As a result, Fard's theology could not strictly be described as Muslim. Rather, as one historian puts it, Fard offered his followers "a veritable hodge-podge of religious ideas."[51]

Racial Pride and Self-Determination

Politically, too, the Nation of Islam owed much to the Moorish Science Temple. Like Ali, Fard was an eager advocate of racial pride and self-determination. He played up the achievements of African and Middle Eastern peoples throughout history, and he taught that blacks, alone of all the peoples in the world, had been created in Allah's own image. But Fard went further, mixing this pro-black message with bitterly antiwhite invective. In particular, he excoriated whites for their role in enslaving and oppressing African Americans.

To Fard the path to success, both worldly and spiritual, was clear. Blacks, he wrote, "must regain their religion, which is Islam, their language, which is Arabic, and their culture, which is astronomy and higher mathematics."[52] In addition, he asserted, African Americans needed to give up alcohol, gambling, and other immoral behaviors. Moreover, Fard advocated that blacks act in their own interest rather than waiting for whites to offer them help. He instructed blacks to separate themselves from whites as much as possible and to found their own businesses and social welfare institutions to take care of themselves.

The slave heritage of African Americans was also an issue for Fard. In his view blacks could not move forward until they had cast off all reminders of slavery. That meant giving up foods such as cornbread and okra, which had been eaten in the slave South and remained popular among many African Americans. It also meant abandoning family names, which as Fard pointed out had often been assigned by slave owners, and adopting Muslim names in their place.

Elijah Muhammad

Like Ali before him, Fard found a receptive audience in the urban North. The Nation of Islam quickly gained members in several northern cities. Among those who heard and accepted Fard's message was a Detroit auto worker named Elijah Poole, who joined the group after hearing Fard speak one evening in 1931. Taking on the name Elijah Muhammad, Poole quickly became Fard's top assistant. In 1934, when Fard disappeared, Muhammad took over leadership of the organization.

In most respects, Muhammad's theology and goals were the same as Fard's. Muhammad did make some changes, however. Where Fard had merely talked about economic self-sufficiency, Muhammad helped make it a reality. Following the lead of some black Christian churches of the period, he and other black Muslims set up stores, factories, and other businesses, all of them designed to bring money into the black community.

Muhammad's rhetoric changed, too. His rhetoric against whites was even more vehement than Fard's. Muhammad developed a theory that whites were actually devils, created through genetic experimentation by an evil scientist. And his indictment of Christianity was particularly potent. In his eyes Christianity was a morally bankrupt religion eager to corrupt and mislead African Americans. "The Bible is my poor people's graveyard," he wrote. "The truth has been added in and taken out of [it] by the devils, the slavemasters of my people."[53]

Finally, Muhammad made a few theological changes upon taking over the Nation of Islam's leadership. Most notably, he declared that Fard had been no ordinary man, but a manifestation of Allah. That, in turn, meant that Elijah Muhammad himself was a prophet—and therefore worthy of praise. "I bear witness that nothing deserves to be worshipped besides Allah," ran a prayer commonly used by black Muslims during Muhammad's time as

Elijah Muhammad successfully guided the Nation of Islam's development.

leader. "And I bear witness that Mr. Elijah Mhammed [Muhammad] is his servant and apostle."[54]

Under Muhammad's leadership the Nation of Islam was successful. It appealed primarily to poor young men from urban areas, but other African Americans also joined. Through the 1940s and 1950s the organization grew steadily. The Nation of Islam offered particular outreach to prisoners, drug addicts, and others who had been in serious trouble, and it maintained its quasi-Muslim brand of religion. Still, the group had little impact at the time beyond the urban cores where it was most popular.

Civil Rights and Malcolm X

The civil rights movement of the 1960s, though, brought sudden attention to the Nation of Islam. The Christian ministers who organized the movement emphasized integration and believed that changing the attitudes of southern whites was both possible and desirable. The Nation of Islam, however, disagreed. In Elijah Muhammad's opinion, such a strategy assumed the goodness of whites—who, in Muhammad's eyes were far from trustworthy. Muhammad argued that blacks should demand their rights rather than appeal to the consciences of white Americans.

At first, most civil rights activists paid little attention to Muhammad's teachings. But as the struggle wore on and the extent of American racism became clear, the uncompromisingly antiwhite messages of the Nation of Islam began to resonate with many civil rights workers. Concluding that whites would never willingly relinquish power, more and more activists found themselves drawn toward the group. While not all of these people actually joined the Nation of Islam, the interest they showed in the organization helped bring it into the public eye.

The face of the Nation of Islam during this time, however, was not so much Elijah Muhammad as it was a man named Malcolm X. Malcolm had joined the movement after his release from prison in the 1950s and had risen quickly within the organization. By the 1960s he was well known as an outspoken leader who helped spread the message of Islam to African Americans everywhere. Like Muhammad himself, Malcolm practiced an antiwhite, anti-Christian philosophy that appealed to blacks who were already Muslims—and to many others who were not.

But Malcolm's religious perspectives soon began to change. After several political and theological disagreements with Muhammad, he abruptly left the Nation of Islam in 1964. Seeking a deeper connection with his faith, he joined the annual Muslim pilgrimage to the holy city of Mecca, Saudi Arabia, later that year. The journey changed his life. Where he had once advocated separatism and focusing on the needs of African Americans, Malcolm now saw Muslims of all races coming together in peace and united in a common goal. Inspired by his experience, Malcolm dropped the expressly American brand of Islam he had learned in prison and became an orthodox Muslim instead.

Malcolm X became a symbol of the Nation of Islam.

Looking Forward

Upon returning to the United States Malcolm immediately began to broaden the outlook of American Muslims. He began to connect the experiences of African Americans with struggles for human rights elsewhere in the world. In his view it was no longer enough for American Muslims to concentrate solely on improving the lives of African Americans; in contrast, he believed it was now time to reach out to oppressed peoples around the globe. Malcolm was assassinated in early 1965 before he could carry out all that he wanted to do.

Muslim Athletes

Other than Malcolm X, the largest group of some of the most recognizably Muslim Americans have been black athletes. The most notable of these was a boxer who was originally known as Cassius Clay. Born in Kentucky in 1942, Clay made a name for himself not only with his abilities in the boxing ring but also with his flair for self-promotion. In 1964 he won the heavyweight boxing title by defeating Sonny Liston, the previous champion. The following day he announced that he had become a member of the Nation of Islam and was taking the name Muhammad Ali. Ali went on to become an international celebrity and one of the most successful boxers the world has ever seen.

Ali was not the only black athlete to convert. Another more recent boxer, Mike Tyson, has converted to Islam, though unlike Ali he has not changed his name. Kareem Abdul-Jabbar, a star basketball player from the 1960s to the 1980s, was known as Lew Alcindor before joining the Nation of Islam as a young man. Other Muslim basketball players through the years have included Jamaal Wilkes, Zaid Abdul-Aziz, and Mahmoud Abdul-Rauf.

Heavyweight boxing champion Cassius Clay changed his name to Muhammad Ali after joining the Nation of Islam in 1964.

Still, Malcolm's ideas were the future of American Islam. In 1975 Elijah Muhammad died and was succeeded as the head of the Nation of Islam by his son Wallace. Wallace Muhammad made some swift and important changes to the organization. Rejecting his father's emphasis on separatism, he welcomed white Muslims into the group. "There is no black Muslim or white Muslim," he explained; "all are Muslims, all children of God."[55] Wallace Muhammad also introduced his people to orthodox Muslim values and practices, making it clear that joining forces with Muslims worldwide was a priority.

Then, in 1987 Wallace went even further. Believing that the Nation of Islam no longer served a purpose, he dissolved the organization and told his followers to join or form mosques in their own communities. A few resisted; these members, led by a cleric named Louis Farrakhan, eventually formed a new Nation of Islam based on the original ideas of Fard and Elijah Muhammad. The majority of Wallace Muhammad's followers, however, did as he suggested.

Today, Islam remains important within the African American community. The Muslim faith continues to be most popular in urban areas and with young men, particularly those who have been in trouble with drugs or the law. But as before, plenty of African Americans who do not fit this description are devout Muslims. Whether drawn to orthodox mosques or to the uniquely American Nation of Islam, these worshippers find comfort and strength within their Muslim faith. They add immeasurably to the texture of African American religion.

Chapter Five

Religion and Civil Rights

Few social movements are as well remembered today as the civil rights movement of the 1950s and 1960s. Certainly, most Americans of the twenty-first century are familiar with the basic outline of the civil rights struggle. Many know the stories of such figures as Ruby Bridges, a black child who integrated an all-white school in New Orleans, and Martin Luther King Jr., who helped lead protests from 1955 until his assassination in 1968. The successes and failures of the movement are familiar to millions who came of age long after the civil rights era was over.

Accounts of the civil rights movement usually detail the events of the era, but they often overlook the significance of religion in the struggle. In fact, the fight against racial prejudice drew much of its character and strength from the Protestant Christianity practiced in southern black churches of the time. Sometimes the connections between Christianity and the movement were apparent. Many civil rights leaders were ministers, for example, and black churches provided meeting space and volunteers throughout the years of the struggle.

But the role of religion in the civil rights movement went much deeper. The ideals of traditional black Christianity served as a rock for those who challenged discrimination and prejudice against black people. Many civil rights leaders looked to their faith for inspiration and for solace. Activists cited scripture to highlight the righteousness of their struggle. And the well-known refusal of civil rights leaders to engage in violence was drawn in large part from Christian ideals. Without the influence of religion, the civil rights movement would have looked very different indeed.

Before the Movement

The civil rights movement was born of long years of frustration with the laws and customs of the South. Under the system of segregation, practiced across the region from the late nineteenth century well into the 1950s, whites and blacks were frequently separated. Legally, African Americans could not eat in many restaurants, sit in "white" sections of movie theaters, or attend public schools set aside for white children. A doctrine of "separate but equal" prevailed, under which—in theory at least—facilities meant for blacks were just

Segregated schools like this one gave rise to the modern civil rights movement.

as good as those reserved for whites. In reality, though, blacks were not given equal treatment. Compared with all-white schools, for example, schools for African American children were crowded, underfunded, and severely lacking in supplies.

The problems faced by African Americans in the South went deeper than segregation, however. Blacks were often barred from voting, so they had no say in government. Economically, too, most blacks were dependent on whites for their jobs. African Americans who spoke out against prejudice risked being fired in retaliation for their views. Those who continued to speak their minds risked their health and safety. Racist organizations such as the Ku Klux Klan often beat up blacks who did not accept the way things were. Occasionally, they brutally murdered those who dared to question the laws and customs of the South.

The threat of violence was highly effective in muting black protest. That was true even in southern black churches. With some exceptions, southern black preachers of the early 1900s rarely spoke out against discrimination and prejudice. In 1940 black political scientist Ralph Bunche visited Memphis, Tennessee, and was deeply saddened by what he saw. "The Negro preachers of Memphis as a whole have avoided social questions," he wrote of his experience. "They have preached thunder and lightning, fire and brimstone, and Moses out of the bulrushes, but about the economic and political exploitation of local blacks they have remained silent."[56]

The Struggle Begins

That mindset was soon be transformed, however. In the years following World War II black anger and resentment began to rise. African American soldiers who had been instrumental in winning the war were upset when they returned home to prejudice and oppression. Slowly and quietly at first, then more and more openly, they began to agitate for change. At the same time, several black groups started a legal battle to integrate public schools—that is, to open them to whites and blacks alike. In 1954 the Supreme Court ruled in their favor in a landmark case known as *Brown v. Board of Education*. The civil rights movement was under way.

Civil rights quickly assumed enormous importance. From 1954 until about 1970, in fact, the battle for civil rights was con-

Civil Rights Songs

The civil rights movement was known for its protest songs. Marchers and demonstrators frequently sang to lift their spirits and to show their determination. Many of their favorite songs were adapted from African American traditions of sacred music. "We Shall Overcome," for example, was a reworking of a gospel song by C.A. Tindley, and a spiritual called "Keep Your Hand on the Plow" became a protest song known as "Keep Your Eyes on the Prize."

In part, civil rights protestors used these songs because they were familiar. In part, too, they used them because they were appropriate. Many of the themes of the spirituals and gospel songs—notably the subjects of justice, love, and suffering—seemed to reflect the experiences of the civil rights workers. At heart, the sacred music of the black church spoke of eventual triumph in the face of hardship, and that message helped inspire and comfort many civil rights activists too.

stantly in the news. During this time the movement experienced many great successes. The *Brown* decision was one. The passage of the Civil Rights Act in 1964, which outlawed segregation everywhere, was another. Activists provided community services for poor southern blacks and secured voting rights for those who had once been too afraid to register. And the movement contributed many lasting images and moments, such as Martin Luther King's famous "I Have a Dream" speech during the March on Washington in 1963.

At the same time, the movement also suffered bitter setbacks and tragedies. Many whites resented the demands of African American protestors and set out to stop them at any cost. In some places African American children who integrated the public schools were taunted and intimidated by racist mobs. Police in Birmingham, Alabama, turned fire hoses and attack dogs on peaceful protestors. Racists bombed the homes of black leaders and set fire to black-owned stores. And several civil rights organizers, including Martin Luther King, lost their lives to violence.

The African American Religious Experience

In the end, the civil rights movement achieved much—but not nearly what it had hoped to accomplish.

The Bus Boycott

The connection between Christianity and the civil rights movement was evident early on. Even during the 1940s a few black clergy members were already leading a call for civil rights. A black minister named Howard Thurman, for example, spoke out frequently on matters of race throughout the decade. To Thurman, Christianity offered the solution to racial discrimination. "The idea was simple," writes a historian, summing up Thurman's view: "Racism is against Christ's teachings and out of line with being a Christian."[57] Another African American minister, Gordon Blaine Hancock, also led efforts to improve race relations in the South during this time.

Still, Ralph Bunche's criticisms of black pastors remained largely true until 1955. That December, African American seamstress and civil rights advocate Rosa Parks of Montgomery, Alabama, was arrested for refusing to yield her seat on a city bus to a white man. Local civil rights leaders responded by organizing a boycott of the bus system by the city's blacks. For nearly a year, most African Americans in Montgomery refused to ride the buses, an action that cost the bus company a great deal of money. The activists' efforts paid off: Late in 1956 segregation on the city's buses officially came to an end.

More than any previous event, the bus boycott cemented the relationship between Christianity and the movement. The reason was a young minister named Martin Luther King Jr. Born in Atlanta, King had come to Montgomery to serve as pastor of a local church shortly before Parks was arrested. Despite King's youth, local civil rights leaders Jo Ann Robinson and E.D. Nixon knew that he was articulate and well respected. They saw him as a potentially valuable ally in the struggle to integrate the city's bus system.

A few days following Parks's arrest, Nixon asked King if he would serve as a spokesman for those planning the boycott. King was doubtful at first but promised to think it over. "I called him back," Nixon remembered afterwards, "and he said, 'Yeah, Brother Nixon, I'll go along with it.'" Nixon was pleased—in more ways than one. "I'm glad of that," he told King, "because I talked to eighteen other people, [and] I told them to meet at your church at three o'clock."[58]

"This Is a Spiritual Movement"

The leadership of activists such as Robinson and Nixon was essential in starting the bus boycott. And of course success would have been impossible without the commitment of Montgomery's African Americans—and the courage of Parks herself. Nonetheless, King quickly became the public face of the boycott. King worked tirelessly to explain the actions of the city's blacks. He spoke again and again about the evils of segregation, and he helped spread news of the boycott beyond Montgomery and the South.

To King the Montgomery bus boycott was not simply a political issue: It was a deeply spiritual action as well. From the beginning, whenever he spoke about the boycott and the civil rights movement, he used terms and images stemming directly from the Christian tradition. "If we are wrong," King said in one of his first public statements about the boycott, "[then] Jesus of Nazareth was merely a utopian dreamer and never came down to earth." Later in the same speech, King vowed that the activists would fight "until justice runs down like water, and righteousness like a mighty stream"[59]—a reference to the Book of Amos in the Hebrew Bible.

By quoting scripture and bringing Jesus into the discussion, King was defining the civil rights movement as a just and moral struggle with an importance that went beyond the everyday world. As reported in the Bible, King pointed out, Jesus routinely stood with the poor and the downtrodden, not the rich and mighty. Moreover, Jesus had worked for justice and advocated a ministry of love for all. As King saw it, then, the battle for civil rights followed Jesus's principles. Like many other civil rights activists, King believed he was carrying out God's will by challenging segregation in the South.

If the civil rights movement was to be a godly movement, however, that limited the ways in which civil rights protestors could act. As Christian civil rights activists pointed out, followers of Jesus were called upon to love and not to harm. "The religion of Jesus says to the disinherited, 'Love your enemy,'"[60] wrote Howard Thurman. The doctrine of nonviolence was not exclusively Christian—Thurman, King, and others had studied the works of Hindu leader Mahatma Gandhi, who had effectively used nonviolent resistance in India. No matter what its source,

Martin Luther King Jr. defined the civil rights movement as a just and moral struggle.

though, the practice of nonviolence meant responding to aggression, even to bloodshed, without fighting back violently, and in large part civil rights protestors did exactly that.

The decision to adopt nonviolent protest was to some extent practical: The white majority in the South, after all, owned most of the weapons. It was also strategic; images of blacks refusing to fight back against brutality helped the movement win the sympathy of many white northerners. But most important were the teachings of Jesus, which, as King and other Christian leaders understood them, barred civil rights activists from fighting back even when attacked.

King made the Christian underpinnings of the civil rights movement especially clear in a speech he gave in early 1956. "This is a spiritual movement," he explained, "and we intend to keep these things in the forefront." In this speech, too, King underscored the religious justification for nonviolent protest. "It is my firm conviction that to seek to retaliate with violence does nothing but intensify the existence of evil and hate in the universe," he said. "I believe firmly that love is a transforming power that can lift a whole community to new horizons of fair play, good will, and justice."[61]

Black Preachers, Black Churches

Both then and now, King certainly ranks as the best-known black preacher involved with the civil rights movement. But other African American preachers were active in every aspect of the movement. Methodist minister James Lawson, for example, was one of the movement's leading proponents of nonviolence, which he saw as "deeply rooted in the spirituality of Jesus [and] deeply rooted in the spirituality of many of the prophetic stories of the Hebrew Bible."[62] Baptist preacher Fred Shuttlesworth spearheaded the struggle in Birmingham. And Ralph Abernathy, another minister, was one of King's closest friends and advisers.

There were good reasons why so many ministers were involved in the movement. Foremost among these, of course, was their faith. The message of the activists reflected the message of Christianity as many of the preachers understood it. "We come this week to think together, to work together, to pray together and to dedicate ourselves to the task of completing the job which

From left, Reverend King, Reverend Fred Shuttlesworth, and
Reverend Ralph Abernathy discuss civil rights demonstrations at a
1963 press conference.

Lincoln began 100 years ago,"[63] said black minister Benjamin
Mays in a speech to open a 1963 religious conference. For some
preachers it would have been almost impossible *not* to have supported the movement.

The reality of African American life also thrust many preachers
into the forefront of the movement. Most blacks, particularly in the
South, were dependent on whites for their livelihoods. By speaking
out against racism, these blacks risked losing their incomes. Black
ministers, on the other hand, earned their pay from fellow blacks.
They did not have to rely directly on the goodwill of whites to keep
their jobs and homes. That relative independence allowed them to
take a more assertive stance for civil rights.

Black congregations played important roles during the civil rights era, too. Mount Zion Church in Longdale, Mississippi, was one of dozens of black churches that agreed to host a "freedom school"—a place where African Americans could learn to stand up for their rights. In Birmingham the Sixteenth Street Baptist Church provided meeting space and a safe haven during the city's many demonstrations, which often took place in a nearby park. Black churches, of course, had long been at the center of the African American community, so being at the center during the civil rights era was nothing new.

The visibility of black preachers and congregations in the movement, however, meant that they were frequent targets of white anger. Birmingham minister Fred Shuttlesworth, for example, was severely beaten many times as he led demonstrations.

Terror on Sixteenth Street

███

September 15, 1963, was to be a special day at the all-black Sixteenth Street Baptist Church in Birmingham, Alabama. The main service that Sunday had been set aside to honor the young people of the church. Shortly before the service, five participants—all girls—went into a restroom to touch up their hair and adjust their clothing. But as they stood at the mirrors, an explosion ripped through the building. A bomb below an outside stairwell had gone off. Four of the girls were killed; the fifth was badly wounded. It was one of the most appalling acts of violence during the civil rights movement.

Evidence soon suggested that the bomb had been set by Ku Klux Klan members hoping to terrorize civil rights workers. Bringing the criminals to justice, however, proved extremely difficult. Though evidence against several of the Klansmen was strong, racism in the state made it unlikely that a jury would vote to convict them—even if local law enforcement agents were willing to bring charges. In the end, three suspects were convicted of murder, but not until decades had passed. The last of the three was not sent to prison until 2002.

Four girls died in a bomb blast at the Sixteenth Street Baptist Church in Birmingham, Alabama in 1963.

Upon being told that Shuttlesworth had been taken to the hospital by ambulance after one such beating, a white city official remarked "I'm sorry I missed it. I wish they'd carried him away in a hearse."[64] Mount Zion Church was burned to the ground shortly after the congregation voted to set up the freedom school; it was one of at least twenty-four black churches in Mississippi destroyed during the summer of 1964 alone. The previous year, a bomb set off at the Sixteenth Street Baptist Church killed four girls and seriously injured another.

The attacks on black preachers and churches were intended to damage more than people and property. The segregationists who carried them out were well aware of the role that faith played in African American life. By attacking black religion, whites hoped to strike a severe blow against the institution that more than any other supported and defined African Americans. They believed that violence against ministers and churches would intimidate civil rights activists and make them give up their cause. But they were wrong. If anything, the attacks on black religion strengthened the activists' resolve. For many civil rights workers, the attacks on clergymen and houses of worship indicated the degree of evil in the segregationist camp—and made it that much more important to struggle on.

More than Christianity

Despite the Christian underpinnings of the civil rights movement, the struggle for black equality was in no way strictly Christian. Thousands of Jews, Muslims, and others with no religious affiliation took part in the movement. These men and women were inspired to act not by their understanding of Jesus but by other factors, spiritual and secular alike. Many non-Christian participants played especially notable roles in the movement. Malcolm X, of course, was a member of the Nation of Islam when he rose to prominence as an activist, and Michael Schwerner, a social worker and organizer who was murdered in Mississippi in 1964, was an atheist who grew up in a Jewish household.

Nor did all Christians support the movement. That was most obviously true of white southerners, many of whom attended church regularly yet had no trouble reconciling a segregationist viewpoint with Christianity. It was also true of many blacks.

Some black preachers agreed with the movement's overall goals, but worried that it did not show enough respect for law and order. "The disrespect for law in the move for freedom has opened the way for criminals to come into our midst,"[65] insisted Baptist minister Joseph H. Jackson. Others questioned the role of black churches in the movement; they argued that ministers should focus not on political action but on the saving of souls.

At the other extreme, the movement's emphasis on pacifism also troubled some African American Christians. These men and women often applauded the concept in theory but found it difficult to support in practice. Albert B. Cleage, a minister in Detroit, was in this camp. "Negroes lack the indignation that people should have in the face of injustice,"[66] Cleage once remarked. Ar-

"I Have a Dream"

Martin Luther King's "I Have a Dream" speech ranks as one of the best-known speeches in American history. Delivered in 1963 during the March on Washington, the speech, like many others given by King, was both secular and religious. Throughout the speech he moved seamlessly from the language of politics to the language of faith. For example, King cited not only the Declaration of Independence but also the Book of Isaiah in the Hebrew Bible. He spoke of the importance of democratic traditions—and talked of the glory of God.

The conclusion of King's speech, in particular, combined images of Christianity with the worldly goals of the civil rights movement. "When we let freedom ring," he said, "when we let it ring from every village and every hamlet, from every state and every city, we will be able to speed up that day when all God's children, black men and white men, Jews and Gentiles, Protestants and Catholics, will be able to join hands and sing in the words of that old Negro spiritual, 'Free at last! Free at last! Thank God almighty, we are free at last!'"

Quoted in Harvard Sitkoff, *The Struggle for Black Equality.* New York: Hill and Wang, 1981, p. 152.

guing that King and his followers should encourage African Americans to stand up for themselves, Cleage found himself drawn instead to the more militant teachings of Malcolm X. He and other Christian thinkers provided an important counterpoint to the ideas of mainstream civil rights leaders.

Nonetheless, Christianity played an essential role in the civil rights movement. Christian principles of love, brotherhood, and justice formed a framework for the movement and inspired thousands of civil rights workers to act as they did. The teachings of Jesus, as understood by King and other civil rights leaders, served as a foundation for the work the activists felt called upon to do. The movement made heavy use of biblical themes and Christian images, and the activists' hope of a brighter future was often an outgrowth of their religious faith. As King wrote in his 1963 "Letter from a Birmingham Jail," "We will win our freedom because the sacred heritage of our nation and the eternal will of God are embodied in our echoing demands."[67]

African American Religion Today

African American religion has evolved substantially throughout American history, and the years since the civil rights movement have been no exception. Yet despite the changes brought by the last few decades, African American religion has continued to thrive. Houses of worship still provide inspiration and comfort for millions of American blacks, and worship still stands at the center of many African American lives. African Americans of faith routinely take part in outreach programs that provide food, shelter, and education to the neediest in their communities. Black members of the clergy speak out against racism, addiction, and violence, and continue to fill the spirits and souls of their congregations by word and deed. While the role of black religious institutions may have changed, the fundamental importance of religion itself to African Americans has not.

New Churches, New Affiliations

One obvious change since the civil rights movement has involved the traditional black church. In the past, as Perry puts it, the church was "the only game in town."[68] During much of the nineteenth and early twentieth centuries, very few blacks were affiliated with any other religious institution. While there were occasional black Episcopalians, Presbyterians, and Roman Catholics—and later, some black Muslims—the overwhelming majority of churchgoing African Americans belonged to historically black congregations.

Black churches continue to thrive today, but they are no longer the only option for twenty-first-century African Americans. In a nation that has become less strictly divided along racial lines, African American Christians are increasingly likely to join congregations that include whites as well as blacks. The number of black Roman Catholics has grown since the 1960s, for instance, and some evangelical churches attract members of both races. According to one scholar, about 10 to 20 percent of African American Christians

Black churches continue to thrive but blacks today have many options for worship. Here, a mixed race crowd takes part in a Roman Catholic Mass.

today are members of institutions unconnected to the traditional black church.

Islam, too, continues to grow in popularity among many blacks. As has been true in the past, some blacks find Islam particularly attractive because, unlike Christianity, it is not closely associated with Europe. The connection of Islam with Africa and the Middle East therefore appeals to blacks who are eager to distance themselves from white culture. The life of Malcolm X has been inspirational for many African Americans, too, and some have sought to emulate him by adopting his Muslim religion. Whatever the reasons, the rise in Islam has cut into the number of people who belong to historically black churches.

Society and Government

Other changes have been sparked by society and government. Once, churches and mosques served as the central nervous systems of their communities. They were the main source of news and information for many African Americans. Today, however, the development of the Internet, cell phones, and satellite television has revolutionized the way Americans communicate. As a result, most blacks no longer rely on religious institutions to provide and interpret the news as was common years ago.

New ideas in government have brought about changes in black religion as well. For many years government provided little help to poor blacks—or, for that matter, to anyone else. Needy African Americans sought assistance instead from private sources, which often meant from black churches. The civil rights movement, however, helped spur the federal government to attack poverty and other social problems. While government aid has by no means succeeded in eliminating these issues, many government programs do offer help to people in need. These programs have tended to reduce the importance of black churches in helping disadvantaged African Americans.

Finally, changes in African American life have affected black churches. On the one hand, more blacks than ever have moved into the middle class and beyond. Many large companies are owned or run by blacks, and thousands of African Americans work as college professors, doctors, and government officials. Many of these most successful men and women do not identify

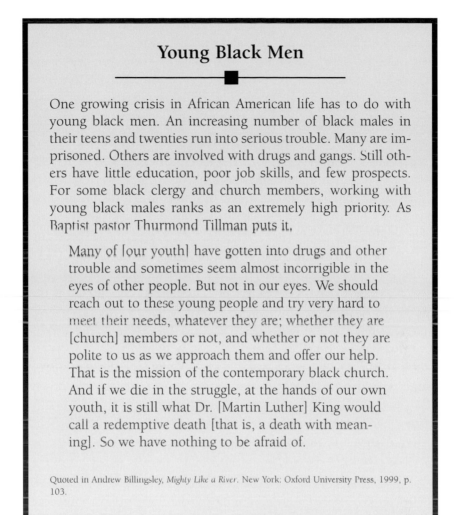

Young Black Men

One growing crisis in African American life has to do with young black men. An increasing number of black males in their teens and twenties run into serious trouble. Many are imprisoned. Others are involved with drugs and gangs. Still others have little education, poor job skills, and few prospects. For some black clergy and church members, working with young black males ranks as an extremely high priority. As Baptist pastor Thurmond Tillman puts it,

> Many of [our youth] have gotten into drugs and other trouble and sometimes seem almost incorrigible in the eyes of other people. But not in our eyes. We should reach out to these young people and try very hard to meet their needs, whatever they are; whether they are [church] members or not, and whether or not they are polite to us as we approach them and offer our help. That is the mission of the contemporary black church. And if we die in the struggle, at the hands of our own youth, it is still what Dr. [Martin Luther] King would call a redemptive death [that is, a death with meaning]. So we have nothing to be afraid of.

Quoted in Andrew Billingsley, *Mighty Like a River*. New York: Oxford University Press, 1999, p. 103.

themselves primarily as black. To them, race does not seem the insurmountable barrier it was in the 1940s or 1950s. These blacks often see themselves as a part of an interracial world in which distinctively African American institutions, such as the black church, have less importance.

At the same time, the experiences of black business leaders and college professors are not reflective of all African Americans. As the overall wealth of the nation rises, conditions in some urban black neighborhoods, in particular, are not improving at all. By one measure, about one-quarter of all American blacks were living in poverty in 2005. For many of these people, moreover, there seems to be little hope of advancement. Drugs, violence, and a lack of job and educational opportunities make it difficult for young African Americans to succeed. All too often they make it difficult even to survive: Violent death rates for young black men are far higher than for men of any other race.

New Challenges

These changes have brought new challenges to African Americans of faith, whether they are members of traditional black Christian churches or not. As in the past, religious institutions have responded to the challenges. Many Islamic mosques, for instance, have established prison ministries designed to help the thousands of African Americans, mostly men, who are behind bars. These ministries offer religious instruction, but they also provide practical support. Many of them, for example, help convicts find jobs and housing upon their release.

Social issues such as drugs and gang violence are not new to American cities, but they have taken on new importance in recent years. While some government programs try to tackle these problems, urban black churches often find themselves better equipped to do so. Pastors and church members frequently live in or near these communities themselves and see the effects of crime, drugs, and disease firsthand. A Louisiana congregation, for instance, bought two crack houses across the street from its church, tore them down, and converted them to low-income housing. Similarly, the New Birth Missionary Baptist Church in Atlanta has trained hundreds of volunteers to educate community members about AIDS prevention.

The emphasis on new challenges does not mean, however, that black religious institutions are ignoring traditional social concerns. On the contrary, economic self-sufficiency and other similar issues remain high priorities for many churches. "We believe that our churches have an obligation to do some things that will strengthen the economic standing of the black community," says Baptist minister Walter Malone. Racism, Malone notes, remains a problem in American society. "There are some things black people have to do for themselves," he adds, "or they will never be done."[69]

Yet despite the value of these and other outreach programs, churches and mosques are fundamentally houses of worship. As has been the case throughout the history of African America, these buildings are more than stone and brick: They are sacred places where ordinary people come to give thanks and praise to their God. Like the black churches of the Great Migration, they provide a home and a safe haven in an uncertain world. Like the Islamic organizations of the twentieth century, black religious institutions of today offer worshippers an opportunity to come together in fellowship and solidarity. And like the black churches of the South during the civil rights movement, these houses of worship inspire their members to go and follow the paths of charity, justice, and righteousness.

A prison mosque at Rikers Island prison in New York ministers to African American inmates.

Throughout the course of African American history, from the earliest days of slavery to urban decay in the late 1900s, religion has played a major role. It has supported and comforted, motivated and led. It has permeated and influenced every aspect of African American life. Religion has always been in the forefront of black Americans' lives and labors. Just as their predecessors have done for several centuries, twenty-first-century African Americans will no doubt continue to draw on their faith to help them attack the problems of today and the future. As a commentator writes, quoting a 1960s gospel song, "Black Americans have come 'this far by faith,' and that faith will remain when all else has fallen away."[70]

Notes

Introduction: Black History, Black Religion

1. Quoted in Gwendolen Sims Warren, *Ev'ry Time I Feel the Spirit.* New York: Henry Holt, 1997, p. 93.
2. Quoted in Albert J. Raboteau, *African-American Religion.* New York: Oxford University Press, 1999, p. 132.

Chapter One: Slave Religion

3. Quoted in Raboteau, *African-American Religion*, p. 17.
4. Quoted in Peter Kolchin, *American Slavery.* New York: Hill and Wang, 1993, p. 54.
5. Quoted in Kolchin, *American Slavery*, p. 55.
6. Quoted in Kolchin, *American Slavery*, p. 55.
7. Raboteau, *African-American Religion*, p. 24.
8. Quoted in Ira Berlin, *Many Thousands Gone.* Cambridge, MA: Harvard University Press, 1998, p. 139.
9. Quoted in Raboteau, *African-American Religion*, p. 49.
10. Quoted in Eugene Genovese, *Roll, Jordan, Roll: The World the Slaves Made.* New York: Pantheon, p. 267.
11. Quoted in Kolchin, *American Slavery*, pp. 144–45.
12. Quoted in Gilbert Osofsky, ed., *Puttin' On Ole Massa.* New York: Harper and Row, 1969, p. 31.
13. Quoted in B.A. Botkin, ed., *Lay My Burden Down: A Folk History of Slavery.* Chicago: University of Chicago Press, 1945, p. 26.
14. Quoted in Kolchin, *American Slavery*, p. 147.

Chapter Two: The Rise of the Black Church

15. Dwight Perry, *Breaking Down Barriers.* Grand Rapids, MI: Baker, 1998, p. 7.
16. Quoted in George F. Bragg, *History of the Afro-American Group of the Episcopal Church*, p. 48. http://docsouth.unc.edu/church/bragg/bragg.html.
17. Quoted in Bragg, *History of the Afro-American Group*, p. 65.
18. Quoted in C. Eric Lincoln and Lawrence H. Mamiya, *The Black Church in the African American Experience.* Durham, NC: Duke University Press, 1990, pp. 49–50.
19. Quoted in PBS, "The Causes and Motives for Establishing St. Thomas's African Church," *Africans in America.* www.pbs.org/wgbh/aia/part3/3h1588t.html.
20. Lincoln and Mamiya, *The Black Church*, p. 52.

21. Quoted in Raboteau, *African-American Religion*, p. 37.

22. Quoted in Raboteau, *African-American Religion*, p. 70.

23. Perry, *Breaking Down Barriers*, p. 112.

24. Quoted in PBS, "God Is a Negro," *This Far by Faith*. www.pbs.org/thisfarbyfaith/transcript/episode_2.pdf.

25. Quoted in Raboteau, *African-American Religion*, p. 77.

26. Quoted in Perry, *Breaking Down Barriers*, p. 45.

27. Quoted in Lincoln and Mamiya, *The Black Church*, p. 120.

28. Perry, *Breaking Down Barriers*, p. 52.

29. Quoted in Lincoln and Mamiya, *The Black Church*, p. 81.

30. Quoted in Eric Robinette and Ken-Yon Hardy, "Finding a Place for Faith in Black Churches," *Middletown Journal,* February 11, 2007. www.middletownjournal.com/n/content/oh/story/news/local/2007/02/11/mj021107black churches.html.

Chapter Three: Black Sacred Music

31. Warren, *Ev'ry Time I Feel the Spirit*, p. 5.

32. Lincoln and Mamiya, *The Black Church*, p. 346.

33. James Weldon Johnson and J. Rosamond Johnson, *The Books of American Negro Spirituals*. New York: Viking, 1940, p. 33.

34. Johnson and Johnson, *The Books of American Negro Spirituals*, p. 33.

35. Quoted in Stephen Currie, *Music in the Civil War*. Cincinnati: Betterway, 1992, p. 92.

36. Quoted in Warren, *Ev'ry Time I Feel the Spirit*, p. 68.

37. Quoted in Johnson and Johnson, *The Books of American Negro Spirituals*, p. 71.

38. Quoted in Warren, *Ev'ry Time I Feel the Spirit*, p. 65.

39. Quoted in Perry, *Breaking Down Barriers*, p. 85.

40. Quoted in Warren, *Ev'ry Time I Feel the Spirit*, p. 154.

41. Quoted in Anthony Heilbut, *The Gospel Sound*. New York: Limelight, 1997, p. xvi.

42. Perry, *Breaking Down Barriers*, p. 92.

43. Quoted in PBS, "People of Faith: Thomas Dorsey," *This Far by Faith*. www.pbs.org/thisfarbyfaith/people/thomas_dorsey.html.

44. Quoted in Norma Jean Lutz, *The History of the Black Church*. Philadelphia: Chelsea House, 2001, p. 90.

45. Quoted in Heilbut, *The Gospel Sound*, p. xxix.

46. Quoted in Warren, *Ev'ry Time I Feel the Spirit*, p. 271.

47. Warren, *Ev'ry Time I Feel the Spirit*, pp. 10–11.

Chapter Four: African American Islam

48. Quoted in Raboteau, *African-American Religion*, p. 54.

49. Juan Williams and Quinton Dixie, *This Far by Faith*. New York:

HarperCollins, 2003, p. 58.

50. Quoted in Aminah Beverly Mc-Cloud, *African American Islam*. New York: Routledge, 1995, p. 12.

51. Louis A. DeCaro Jr., *Malcolm and the Cross*. New York: New York University Press, 1998, p. 15.

52. Quoted in Williams and Dixie, *This Far by Faith*, p. 188.

53. Quoted in DeCaro, *Malcolm and the Cross*, p. 46.

54. Quoted in DeCaro, *Malcolm and the Cross*, p. 39.

55. Quoted in Lincoln and Mamiya, *The Black Church*, p. 390.

Chapter Five: Religion and Civil Rights

56. Quoted in Nick Salvatore, *Singing in a Strange Land*. New York: Little, Brown, 2005, p. 56.

57. Williams and Dixie, *This Far by Faith*, p. 205.

58. Quoted in James Oliver Horton and Lois E. Horton, *Hard Road to Freedom: The Story of African America*. New Brunswick, NJ: Rutgers University Press, 2001, p. 281.

59. Quoted in Raboteau, *African-American Religion*, p. 111.

60. Quoted in Williams and Dixie, *This Far by Faith*, p. 206.

61. Quoted in Williams and Dixie, *This Far by Faith*, pp. 215–16.

62. Quoted in Williams and Dixie, *This Far by Faith*, p. 226.

63. Quoted in Mark L. Chapman, *Christianity on Trial*. Maryknoll, NY: Orbis, 1996, p. 40.

64. Quoted in Juan Williams, *Eyes on the Prize*. New York: Penguin, 1987, p. 191.

65. Quoted in Salvatore, *Singing in a Strange Land*, p. 230.

66. Quoted in Salvatore, *Singing in a Strange Land*, p. 266.

67. Quoted in Horton and Horton, *Hard Road to Freedom*, p. 290.

Afterword: African American Religion Today

68. Perry, *Breaking Down Barriers*, p. 23.

69. Quoted in Andrew Billingsley, *Mighty Like a River*. New York: Oxford University Press, 1999, p. 164.

70. Williams and Dixie, *This Far by Faith*, p. 298.

For More Information

Books

B.A. Botkin, ed., *Lay My Burden Down: A Folk History of Slavery.* Chicago: University of Chicago Press, 1945. Recollections of former slaves interviewed years after the Civil War. Endlessly fascinating for many reasons, not least for the information it provides on slave religion.

Stephen Currie, *Life of a Slave on a Southern Plantation.* San Diego: Lucent, 2000. Describes the daily lives of southern slaves during the first half of the nineteenth century; includes information on religious traditions as well as useful background information for slavery.

James Oliver Horton and Lois E. Horton, *Hard Road to Freedom: The Story of African America.* New Brunswick, NJ: Rutgers University Press, 2001. A long but informative history of African Americans from the earliest days of slavery to the end of the twentieth century.

Alan Lomax, *Folk Songs of North America.* New York: Doubleday, 1960. A collection of American songs, including many from the African American religious tradition. Provides words, music, and commentary.

Norma Jean Lutz, *The History of the Black Church.* Philadelphia: Chelsea House, 2001. A short but interesting account of the black church from its beginnings to the 2000s. Includes photographs and other illustrations.

Aminah Beverly McCloud, *African American Islam.* New York: Routledge, 1995. This volume describes the various strands of African American Islamic movements, from the early 1900s to today. Provides information on Noble Drew Ali, Elijah Muhammad, and Malcolm X.

Dwight Perry, *Breaking Down Barriers.* Grand Rapids, MI: Baker, 1998. Perry is a professor of religious studies and a former pastor. This book describes the structure, history, and outreach of American black churches.

Albert J. Raboteau, *African-American Religion.* New York: Oxford University Press, 1999. A thorough and engrossing account of African American religious thought through the years. Places African American religion in a detailed historic context throughout. Raboteau is a scholar known for his research and writing on black religion.

Gwendolen Sims Warren, *Ev'ry Time I Feel the Spirit*. New York: Henry Holt, 1997. Warren, a professional musician and music minister, provides music and lyrics to a number of well-known spirituals, gospel songs, and hymns sung over time by African Americans. She includes valuable commentary on African American music as well.

Juan Williams, *Eyes on the Prize*. New York: Penguin, 1987. Describes the civil rights movement. Includes plenty of pictures and many first-hand accounts of people who were involved in the struggle for racial equality.

Juan Williams and Quinton Dixie, *This Far by Faith*. New York: HarperCollins, 2003. A companion volume to a television series broadcast on PBS. A long and detailed description of African American religion over time. Emphasizes stories of important people within black religious history.

Web Sites

Africans in America (www.pbs.org/ wgbh/aia/home.html). The Web site of the PBS series *Africans in America* offers documents, commentary, and links relating to the history of blacks in North America through the Civil War. Includes information on slave religion, black music, and the founding of African American churches.

The Black Church Page (www.the blackchurchpage.com). A clearinghouse for information, news articles, and links relating to black churches in the United States, with an emphasis on what is happening in African American churches today.

Eyes on the Prize (www.pbs.org/ wgbh/amex/eyesontheprize). The Web site of a PBS television series about the civil rights movement. Provides some information about the religious underpinnings of the struggle for civil rights.

This Far by Faith (www.pbs.org/this farbyfaith). The Web site of a PBS television series about the religious journey of African Americans from early slave times to the present. Music, African American Islam, and the development of the black church are all discussed in detail on this site.

Index

A

Abdul-Jabbar, Kareem (Lew Alcindor), 70
Abernathy, Ralph, 79
Abyssinian Baptist Church (New York), 43
African Americans
civil rights movement and, 10–11
religion and, 13
young men, , 89
African Methodist Episcopal (AME) Church, 33
Ali, Muhammad (Cassius Clay), 70
Ali, Noble Drew, 61–63
Allen, Richard, 31–32, 38
AME Zion Church, 33–34

B

Bethel Church (Philadelphia), 32
Bible
antislavery argument, 23
slavery in, 19
Black church
African-American life and, 88–89
modern, 87
rise of, 29
role of, in South, 37–38
sermons in, 54
social issues addressed by, 12, 90–91
Brewster, W.H., 47
Brown v. Board of Education (1954), 74, 75
Bunch, Ralph, 74, 76

C

Campbell, Lucie, 52
Canaanite Temple (Newark), 62
Chesnut, Mary, 25, 26
Christianity
civil rights movement and, 72–73, 77, 85
making slaves obedient, 21–22
practice of, 23–25
reluctance to introduce slaves to, 19, 21
view of, 63
Civil rights movement, 10, 72–73
black churches involved in, 79–81
government action spurred by, 88
Nation of Islam and, 68
setbacks in, 75–76
songs of, 75
Cleage, Albert B., 42, 84, 85

D

Dane Ministry Institute, 56
Dixie, Quinton, 59
Dixie Hummingbirds, 53
Dorsey, Thomas, 51

E

Education, 34
Ellington, Duke, 55

F

Fard, W.D. (Wali Fard Muhammad), 64–66

Farrakan, Louis, 71
First African Baptist Church, 35

G
Gandhi, Mahatma, 77
God, 25–26
Gospel music, 50–52
Great Awakening, 21–22
Great Migration, 38–39
  gospel music and, 51–52
  role of black church in, 41–43

H
Hancock, Gordon Blaine, 76
Hite, Elizabeth Ross, 12

I
I Have a Dream speech (King), 84
Islam, 57
  development of, 59
  growth in popularity of, 87–88
  revival of, among blacks, 60–63

J
Jackson, Joseph H., 84
Jackson, Mahalia, 53, 54
Jamestown colony, 14
Jesus
  portrayal of, 42
  teachings of, 85
  white *vs.* slave view of, 25–26
Jews, black, 57
Johnson, James Weldon, 46
Jones, Absalom, 31, 38

K
Kee, John P., 55
King, Martin Luther, Jr., 72, 75, 85
  on civil rights movement, 79

  Montgomery bus boycott and, 76, 77
Ku Klux Klan, 74, 81

L
Lawson, James, 79
Lee, Jarena, 39
Letter from a Birmingham Jail (King), 85
Liele, George, 35
Lincoln, C. Eric, 45
Liston, Sonny, 70
Lynch, James, 36

M
Malcolm X, 68–70, 83, 88
Malone, Walter, 91
Mamiya, Lawrence, 45
Martin, Roberta, 53
Mays, Benjamin, 80
McKim, Lucy, 46
Montgomery bus boycott, 76–77
Moorish Science Temple (Newark), 62
Mount Zion Church (Longdale, MS),
  81, 83
Muhammad, Elijah (Elijah Poole),
  66–67, 68
Muhammad, Wallace, 71
Music, 75
Muslims
  among West Africans, 16
  black, 57

N
Nat Turner's rebellion, 27
Nation of Islam, 63–65
  civil rights movement and, 68
  under Elijah Muhammad, 66–67
  Louis Farrakan and, 71
Nixon, E.D., 76, 77
North

gospel music and, 51–52
growth of black churches in, 30–34

O
Olivet Baptist Church (Chicago), 13

P
Parks, Rosa, 76
Pentecostalism, 42
  gospel music and, 52–53
Perry, Dwight, 29, 41, 86
Protestantism, 22–23

R
Racism
  as continuing problem, 91
  in South, 74
Rahman, Ibrahima Abdul, 60
Religion, African-American, forms of,
  12
Rituals
  in Christianity, 26
  of traditional African religions, 18
Robinson, Jo Ann, 76, 77
Roboteau, Robert, 22
Roman Catholics, black, increase in,
  87

S
Sacred music, 44
  African traditions and, 45–46
  European hymns, 49–50
  gospel, 50–52
  in modern black worship, 55–56
  spirituals, 46–49
Said, Omar ibn, 59
Santeria, 62
Schwerner, Michael, 84
Shuttlesworth, Fred, 79, 81, 83

Sixteenth Street Baptist Church
  (Birmingham), 81, 83
Slavery
  American system of, 8–9
  ending of, 10
  heritage of, 65–66
Slaves
  attitudes on Christianizing, 19,
    21–22
  Christianity as practiced by, 23–25
  colonial era, 14–16
  Muslim, 59–60
  religious expression among, 18
  spirituals and worship by, 49
South
  resistance to black congregations in,
    34–35
  rise of black churches in, 35–37
  segregation in, 73–74
Spirituals, 46–49
  gospel music vs., 50–51
St. George Methodist Church
  (Philadelphia), 30–31
St. Thomas Church (Philadelphia),
  31

T
Taylor, Henry, 37
Thurman, Howard, 76, 77
Tillman, Thurmond, 89
Tindley, C.A., 51, 75
Truth, Sojourner, 39
Tubman, Harriet, 25
Turner, Henry, 42
Turner, Nat, 27
Turner, Tina, 57
Tyson, Mike, 70

W
Walker, Alice, 57
West Africans, religions of,
  16–18
White, George, 27–28
Williams, Juan, 59

Williams, Marion, 53
Women, 39
Wright, Richard, 43

Y
Yorba people, deity of, 16–17

Picture Credits

Cover: © Bob Sacha/CORBIS
AP Images, 50, 53, 64, 67, 70, 80, 82, 87, 91
The Art Archive/Culver Pictures, 20
Cameraphoto Arte, Venice/Art Resource, N.Y., 24
National Portrait Gallery, Smithsonian Institution/Art Resource, N.Y., 30
Schomburg Center/Art Resource, N.Y., 33
© Bettmann/CORBIS, 17
© Angelo Hornak/CORBIS, 35
© Bob Sacha/CORBIS, 45
© Underwood & Underwood/CORBIS, 41
© CORBIS, 40
© John Van Hasselt/CORBIS SYGMA, 58
American School/The Bridgeman Art Library/Getty Images, 27
Alfred Eisenstaedt/Time & Life Pictures/Getty Images, 36
Kean Collection/Getty Images, 32
Robert Parent/Time & Life Pictures/Getty Images, 69
Howard Sochurek/Time & Life Pictures/Getty Images, 78
© Syracuse Newspapers/The Image Works, 61
Library of Congress, 9, 56, 73
© North Wind Picture Archives, 11, 15, 28, 48

About the Author

Stephen Currie has written many books and educational materials for young adults on subjects ranging from slavery to piano manufacture and from exploration to Wild West shows. He lives with his family in New York State. Among his interests are reading, kayaking, and hiking.